# THE BOOK OF OBADIAH

# THE BOOK OF OBADIAH

by

DON W. HILLIS

Associate Director
The Evangelical Alliance Mission

BAKER BOOK HOUSE
Grand Rapids, Michigan

Library of Congress Catalog Card Number: 68-19687

PRINTED IN THE UNITED STATES OF AMERICA

# DEDICATION

To the man and woman who questions the awesome power of hate; to Christians who become cynical when the wicked prosper, and to suffering people who wonder whether justice will ever prevail, I dedicate this commentary on OBADIAH.

D.W.H.

# CONTENTS

# OUTLINES OF OBADIAH

## I

1. The Doom of Eden, vv. 1-16
2. The Deliverance of the Chosen People, vv. 17-21
   — According to F. C. Thompson

## II

1. Edom's Destination Foretold, vv. 1-9
2. Cause of Edom's Fall, vv. 10-14
3. The Day of the Lord, vv. 15-21
   — According to M. F. Unger

## III

1. Divine Judgment upon Edom, vv. 1-4
2. Edom's Doom Portrayed in Advance, vv. 5-7
3. Failure of the Wise and Strong, vv. 8-10
4. Edom's Treachery and Its Requital in the Day of the Lord, vv. 11-15
5. Death and New Life from the Holy Hill, vv. 16-18
6. The Kingdom of God, vv. 19-21
   — According to J. H. Eaton

## IV

1. The Certainty of Judgment, vv. 1-9
2. The Cause of Judgment, vv. 10-16
3. The Consummation of Judgment, vv. 17-21

# Chapter I

## OBADIAH JOINS THE PROPHETS

The thirty-first book of the Old Testament contains only twenty-one verses and is the shortest of the thirty-nine books. The fact of its brevity has probably caused many to neglect a study of it. This is regrettable. The child of God cannot afford to neglect the study of any book of the Bible.

In his book, *Israel's Prophets*, Petrie defends the brevity of Obadiah. He says, "The costly and most radiant gems are often strung on the shortest thread. Among the larger jewels of God's Word, this little jewel has its worth."

Telegrams are noted for their brevity and for the significance of their message. This is one of God's "telegrams" and we shall discover that it has many lessons to teach us not only prophetically but also by way of spiritual application. But before we begin a study of the content of Obadiah's book, we need to consider the spirit in which it was written.

It is not unlikely that this unidentifiable prophet of God (see chap. III) was a refugee living under the severest of conditions. He did not, however, allow this to make him bitter of spirit. Though the judgments he predicts are severe, they flow out of a tender heart. It is not difficult to observe, for example, the difference between the tone of Obadiah's prophecy against Edom and Ezekiel's prophecy.

George Petrie speaks highly of the quality of Obadiah's character. He says Obadiah tells of the doom of Edom, "but he does not exult in it. As he sees his proud foes stagger under the weight of divine judgment, his heart is filled with pity and he says: 'Thou shouldest not have provoked Jehovah's wrath.' Magnanimous exile! He wears the fetters which Edom helped to forge. He bows beneath the burden which Edom helped to increase. He endures the weight of sorrows, for which Edom clapped her hands and laughed with fiendish delight. But he turns aside to shed a tear or two when Edom falls."

Not all prophetic teachers would agree with Petrie that

Obadiah was one of Babylon's captives. However, all must agree that Obadiah's circumstances must have been far from comfortable. The entire span of years in which Obadiah lived were dark and depressing. They were years that would nurture any natural tendency toward bitterness. But Obadiah seemed somehow to live above his circumstances.

## Comfort for Israel

His tenderhearted spirit may in part be explained by the motivation of his prophecy. Obadiah's basic purpose in writing the book was not so much to pronounce judgment against Edom as it was to comfort Israel.

Calvin claims that Obadiah "threatened the Idumeans for the sake of administering consolation to the chosen people; for it was a grievous and hard trial for the children of Jacob, an elect people, to see the prosperity of Esau who had been rejected by God, flourishing both in wealth and power.

"Because the children of Israel were miserable in comparison to the Edomites, the adoption of God might have appeared worthless to them. Adversity produces sorrow and weariness, and if the prosperity of others is observed by us, our sorrow is enhanced and our weariness increased. When, therefore, the Israelites saw the Idumeans living in ease and beyond the reach of danger; when they also saw their enjoyment of every abundance while they themselves were exposed and a prey to their enemies, and were continually expecting new calamities, it could not have been, but that their faith must have utterly failed, or at least become much weakened.

"For this reason, the prophet shows that though the Idumeans now lived happily, in a short time they would be destroyed; therefore, they were hated by God; and he shows that this would be the case as we shall see from the contents of this book for the sake of the chosen people."

Someone has said that God's curse pronounced upon Edom is the "implication that breaks forth from the Lamentations of Jeremiah; it is the combination of the fiercest threats of Ezekiel; it is the whole purpose of the short, sharp cry of Obadiah; it is the bitterest drop of sad recollections of the Israelite captive by the waters of Babylon; and the one warlike strain of the evangelical prophet inspired by the hope that the Divine Conqueror would come knee-deep in Idumean blood."

And this He will do. It is from Mount Seir that the blood-stained Divine Warrior comes marching up the ravines and the crags of the valley of the Kidron. The prophet Isaiah says,

> "Who is this that cometh from Edom, with dyed garments from Bozrah? this that is glorious in his apparel, travelling in the greatness of his strength? I that speak in righteousness, mighty to save. Wherefore art thou red in thine apparel, and thy garments like him that treadeth in the winefat? I have trodden the winepress alone; and of the people there was none with me: for I will tread them in mine anger, and trample them in my fury; and their blood shall be sprinkled upon my garments, and I will stain all my raiment. For the day of vengeance is in mine heart, and the year of my redeemed is come" (63:1-4).

## Other Prophets Speak

As is already evident, Obadiah is not alone in his denunciations against the Edomites. It is only right, therefore, that we also listen to the voices of the other prophets.

### Joel

Joel was one of the first prophets to speak against Edom. His prediction was brief but devastating. He says,

> "Egypt shall be a desolation, and Edom shall be a desolate wilderness, for the violence against the children of Judah, because they have shed innocent blood in their land" (3:19).

### Jeremiah

Jeremiah has much to say about God's judgment on Edom and it would appear that he has inculcated some of Obadiah into his pronouncement. Though Bible scholars disagree in regard to this, the majority seem to favor the idea that Obadiah was the earlier of the two writers. Jeremiah says,

> "Concerning Edom, thus saith the Lord of hosts; Is wisdom no more in Teman? is counsel perished from the

prudent? is their wisdom vanished? Flee ye, turn back, dwell deep, O inhabitants of Dedan; for I will bring the calamity of Esau upon him, the time that I will visit him. If grapegatherers come to thee, would they not leave some gleaning grapes? if thieves by night, they will destroy till they have enough. But I have made Esau bare, I have uncovered his secret places, and he shall not be able to hide himself: his seed is spoiled, and his brethren, and his neighbors, and he is not. Leave thy fatherless children, I will preserve them alive; and let thy widows trust in me. For thus saith the Lord; Behold, they whose judgment was not to drink of the cup have assuredly drunken; and art thou he that shall altogether go unpunished? thou shalt not go unpunished, but thou shalt surely drink of it. For I have sworn by myself, saith the Lord, that Bozrah shall become a desolation, a reproach, a waste, and a curse: and all the cities thereof shall be perpetual wastes. I have heard a rumor from the Lord, and an ambassador is sent unto the heathen, saying, Gather ye together, and come against her, and rise up to the battle. For, lo, I will make thee small among the heathen, and despised among men. Thy terribleness hath deceived thee, and the pride of thine heart, O thou that dwellest in the clefts of the rock, that holdest the height of the hill: though thou shouldest make thy nest as high as the eagle, I will bring thee down from thence, saith the Lord. Also Edom shall be a desolation: every one that goeth by it shall be astonished, and shall hiss at all the plagues thereof. As in the overthrow of Sodom and Gomorrah and the neighbor cities thereof, saith the Lord, no man shall abide there, neither shall a son of man dwell in it. Behold, he shall come up like a lion from the swelling of Jordan against the habitation of the strong: but I will suddenly make him run away from her: and who is a chosen man, that I may appoint over her? for who is like me? and who will appoint me the time? and who is that shepherd that will stand before me? Therefore hear the counsel of the Lord, that he hath taken against Edom; and his purposes, that he hath purposed against the inhabitants of Teman: Surely the least of the flock shall draw them out: surely he will make their habitations desolate with them. The earth is moved at the noise of their fall, at the cry the noise thereof was heard in the Red sea. Behold, he shall come up and fly as the eagle, and spread his wings over Bozrah: and at that day shall the heart of the mighty men of Edom be as the heart of a woman in her pangs" (49: 7-22).

Then in Lamentations 4:22, the weeping prophet cries, ". . . He will visit thine iniquity, O daughter of Edom; He will discover thy sins."

### Ezekiel

It is with incisive statements that Ezekiel prophesies God's vengeance on the Edomites. And he makes it plain why that vengeance should fall.

"Thus saith the Lord God; Because that Edom hath dealt against the house of Judah by taking vengeance, and hath greatly offended, and revenged himself upon them; Therefore thus saith the Lord God; I will also stretch out mine hand upon Edom, and will cut off man and beast from it; and I will make it desolate from Teman; and they of Dedan shall fall by the sword. And I will lay my vengeance upon Edom by the hand of my people Israel: and they shall do in Edom according to mine anger and according to my fury; and they shall know my vengeance, saith the Lord God" (25:12-14).

### Amos

Amos proclaims God's judgments upon several of Israel's enemies, and Edom is included.

"Thus saith the Lord; For three transgressions of Edom, and for four, I will not turn away the punishment thereof; because he did pursue his brother with the sword, and did cast off all pity, and his anger did tear perpetually, and he kept his wrath for ever: But I will send a fire upon Teman, which shall devour the palaces of Bozrah" (1:11-12).

### Malachi

Even the last book of the Old Testament has a word for us concerning God's attitude toward Edom.

15

"The burden of the word of the Lord to Israel by Malachi. I have loved you, saith the Lord. Yet ye say, Wherein hast thou loved us? Was not Esau Jacob's brother? saith the Lord: yet I loved Jacob, and I hated Esau, and laid his mountains and his heritage waste for the dragons of the wilderness. Whereas Edom saith, We are impoverished, but we will return and build the desolate places; thus saith the Lord of hosts, they shall build, but I will throw down; and they shall call them, The border of wickedness, and, The people against whom the Lord hath indignation for ever. And your eyes shall see, and ye shall say, The Lord will be magnified from the border of Israel" (1:1-5).

How literally the predictions of these prophets were fulfilled. How devastating and ultimate the judgments of God are upon those who harden their hearts against Him. And how good of God to give men the voices of more than one witness concerning His program. Among them Obadiah has something to say to us.

# Chapter II

## BACKGROUND ON THE BOOK

Obadiah's basic message can be summarized in five easily-understood words: Edom's doom and Israel's glory. When you have said that you have summarized the whole book.

But where is Edom? Who are the Edomites? And why was God's judgment to fall on them? These and other questions must be answered if we are properly to understand Obadiah.

Even a casual reader of Obadiah becomes aware that the prophet is putting his finger on a bitter conflict which has existed between the Edomites and the Israelites. Nor does it take a lot of research to discover that the Edomites are descendants of Esau while the Israelites are descendants of Jacob. In other words, this is the story of an undying animosity between the descendants of twin brothers.

Interestingly enough, the Bible gives us numerous illustrations of brother-brother conflicts — all of them with tragic consequences. There are the conflicts between Cain and Abel, Ishmael and Isaac, and Esau and Jacob. In each case, the older persecuted the younger and the carnal rose up against the spiritual. In each case, God was the final arbitrator.

### Cain and Abel

Cain and Abel were born of fallen parents. They were the first offspring of Adam and Eve after sin entered the world. At the birth of Cain, Eve said, "I have gotten a man from the Lord." She probably felt her newborn babe was the answer to God's promise as given in Genesis 3:15. But how mistaken she was. As Unger suggests in his *Bible Handbook*, "Instead of getting the Saviour, she got a murderer."

In the book of Jude, verse 11, a curse is pronounced on those who have gone in the way of Cain. The way of Cain is the way of the natural man. It stands in bold contrast to the way of the Lord. And it must be remembered that as

17

the heavens are high above the earth, so are His ways above man's ways.

Cain was not one who was ready to accept the necessity of a blood sacrifice for sin. When Abel offered the firstlings of his flocks to the Lord, then the Lord showed "respect unto Abel and his offering," while at the same time rejecting Cain's bloodless offering. This made Cain angry. The Lord reasoned with Cain but to no avail. He rejected the opportunity to repent. Unger suggests that "Cain's religion was too fastidious to kill a lamb, but not too cultured to murder his brother."

This tragic conflict ended in the murder of Abel and the curse of God on Cain. Cain went out from the presence of the Lord and lived the rest of his life in utter independence of God.

On the other hand, it is written of Abel, "By faith Abel offered unto God a more excellent sacrifice than Cain, by which he obtained witness that he was righteous, God testifying of his gifts: and by it he being dead yet speaketh" (Hebrews 11:4).

### Ishmael and Isaac

Ishmael was the son of Abraham by Hagar, Sarah's Egyptian handmaiden. The story is a sad one.

Ten years had passed since God had promised Abraham He would make a great nation of him and would make his name great. In impatience and unbelief, Sarah had encouraged Abraham to have children by Hagar. But conflict arose between Sarah and her Egyptian handmaid the moment she learned that Hagar had conceived. Hagar then fled to the wilderness where the angel of the Lord met her and instructed her to return to her mistress. At the same time the angel of the Lord gave unto Hagar this promise, "I will multiply thy seed exceedingly, that it shall not be numbered for multitude. And the angel of the Lord said unto her, Behold, thou art with child, and shalt bear a son, and shalt call his name Ishmael because the Lord hath heard thy affliction. And he will be a wild man; his hand will be against every man, and every man's hand against him . . ." (Genesis 16:10-12).

History bears irrefutable evidence as to how literally this prophecy concerning Ishmael's descendants has been fulfilled.

Almost fourteen years after the birth of Ishmael, Sarah gave birth to Isaac. Then the bitterness between Sarah and Hagar became unbearable and Hagar and Ishmael were forced to flee. Not, however, before God assured Abraham of two things:

(1) Concerning Ishmael — "Behold, I have blessed him, and will make him fruitful, and will multiply him exceedingly; twelve princes shall he beget, and I will make him a great nation" (Genesis 17:20).

(2) Concerning Isaac — "But my covenant will I establish with Isaac" (Genesis 17:21).

## The Lesson Interpreted

Within these historical facts is an object lesson with a spiritual message. The lesson is interpreted for us by the Spirit of God in the Epistle to the Galatians.

"For it is written, that Abraham had two sons, the one by a bondmaid, the other by a freewoman. But he who was of the bondwoman was born after the flesh; but he of the freewoman was by promise. Which things are an allegory: for these are the two covenants; the one from the mount Sinai, which gendereth to bondage, which is Agar. For this Agar is mount Sinai in Arabia, and answereth to Jerusalem which now is, and is in bondage with her children. But Jerusalem which is above is free, which is the mother of us all. For it is written, Rejoice, thou barren that bearest not; break forth and cry, thou that travailest not: for the desolate hath many more children than she which hath an husband. Now we, brethren, as Isaac was, are the children of promise. But as then he that was born after the flesh persecuted him that was born after the Spirit, even so it is now. Nevertheless what saith the scripture? Cast out the bondwoman and her son: for the son of the bondwoman shall not be heir with the son of the freewoman. So then, brethren, we are not children of the bondwoman, but of the free" (Galatians 4:22-31).

Two great nations came from the loins of Abraham — the Ishmaelites and the Israelites. And it was from among the descendants of Ishmael that Islam was born. Today 450,000,000

19

Moslems adhere to Islam. They firmly believe that Ishmael was the promised offspring of Abraham and that Mohammed was God's long-promised prophet. Islam's interpretation of Deuteronomy 18:15, "The Lord thy God will raise up unto thee a Prophet from the midst of thee, of thy brethren, like unto me; unto him ye shall hearken," has been the great dividing line between Judaism, Islam, and Christianity. Judaism interprets "a Prophet" to mean the coming Messiah, while Christianity finds "a Prophet" fulfilled in Jesus Christ. Both of these stand in opposition to Islam's interpretation.

It would be difficult to estimate the amount of blood that has been shed as a result of the bitter conflicts between the descendants of Ishmael and Isaac. Numerous attempts have been made by each to destroy the other. For almost four thousand years, they have been at each others' throats. Nor is their deadly quarrel over. Israel's newly found statehood and the battles between the Arabs and the Israelites which have followed bring this whole tragic picture into bold focus today. And we can be assured that as long as the Mosque of Omar stands on the reputed site of Solomon's temple the final battle has not been fought nor the last drop of blood shed.

And what shall we say about the long and bloody battles that have taken place between Moslems and Christians. How does one interpret Islam's conquest of much of Europe and North Africa and the responding victories of the Crusaders? Do not these also carry us back to the conflict between the offspring of the "bondwoman" and the "freewoman?"

Yes, the descendants of these half-brothers have bathed the world in blood. They have proven that the basis of murder is hate. Nor is hatred ever hotter than when it grows in the soil of religious convictions.

This brings us to the story of Esau and Jacob — a story to which we are introduced in Genesis. It is a long-continued story whose last chapter was not written until after the crucifixion of Christ.

## Esau and Jacob

We can only understand Obadiah as we understand Esau, for Esau was the father of the Edomites.

It was left to the writer of the book of Hebrews to write Esau's epitaph. He did it under the inspiration of the Spirit in one immensely descriptive word — *profane*. G. Campbell Morgan describes a profane person as one "with no spiritual perception; one who is independent of God . . . proud of his animal ability." And as one reads the account of Esau's life, he is left with the impression that here is indeed a man who had no reverence for the sacred, no relish for the religious and no appetite for the spiritual.

Not once in all of Esau's life did he indicate any desire toward the God of Abraham and Isaac. Esau said no prayers and built no altars. Not once did he ever commune with God and he deliberately and continually behaved in a manner disleasing to God.

This stands in bold contrast to the life of Jacob. With all of Jacob's failures, he recognized spiritual values. He "stumbled after a spiritual ideal" (G. Campbell Morgan). He clung to the God of Abraham and Isaac. He was constantly praying unto God and building altars of worship. With all of his downsittings and uprisings, Bethel and Peniel were sacred to him. There was good soil in Jacob's heart. Though it is true that both tares and wheat grew there, his basic concerns were for the wheat.

It is not to be wondered at that God said, "Jacob have I loved, but Esau have I hated" (Romans 9:13).

### Esau's Life Reviewed

The record of Esau's life is given in six chapters of Genesis: 25-28, 32, and 33. It is the description of a root out of which a nation of cruel people grew. G. Campbell Morgan says, "Edom is Esau enlarged into national life." Esau indeed produced "after his kind." His descendants were irreligious, carnal, and profane.

The Bible introduces us to Esau before he was born, and centuries of tragedy are foreshadowed in that introduction.

Isaac and Rebecca had been married twenty years and were without children. Isaac entreated the Lord for his wife "and Rebecca his wife conceived." We are then told *the children struggled together within her . . ."* (Genesis 25:22). This unpretentious statement introduces us to the first act of one of the saddest dramas of all history. The struggle which began in Rebecca's womb did not end for centuries. Nor can conflicts be more tragic than when they involve blood brothers. Of all wars, civil wars are most to be despised.

When Rebecca inquired of the Lord concerning the struggle taking place within her, the Lord said, "two nations are in thy womb, and two manner of people shall be separated from thy bowels . . ." (Genesis 25:23). These two nations carried on the bitter battle begun in Rebecca's womb. For centuries, these "two manner of people" lived in awful conflict one against the other. The book of Obadiah draws apart the curtains on the final scene of that conflict. It proclaims God's judgment on the descendants of Esau and His blessing on the descendants of Jacob.

At the birth of the twins, we read, "And the first came out red, all over like an hairy garment; and they called his name Esau" (Genesis 25:25).

Of Esau we are told he was a "cunning hunter, a man of the field." Later on his father, Isaac, prophesied of him, "Behold, thy dwelling shall be the fatness of the earth, and of the dew of heaven from above; and by thy sword shalt thou live . . ." (Genesis 27:39, 40). And Esau did indeed become the progenitor of men who lived in the fields and the deserts and who prospered by the power of the sword.

The bitter animosity that existed between Esau and Jacob was heightened when Esau sold his birthright to Jacob for a mess of "red pottage." It was at that time Esau obtained the name Edom, which means *red* (Genesis 25:30). And of Esau it is written that he "despised his birthright" (Genesis 25:34). For one bowl of red pottage, Esau gave up all the sacred rights and privileges that belonged to the firstborn.

The next step in Esau's sojourn from all that is godly and good was his marriage of heathen wives. Genesis 26:34 records his marriage to two Hittite women. Later on he married one of the daughters of Ishmael. He deliberately did this knowing it would displease his father. Parental ideals, religious traditions and even the commands of God were meaningless to this man of the world.

Jacob first bought the birthright from Esau for a mess of pottage and then stole from Esau the blessing of Isaac, his father, through subtlety and deceit. We are told "Esau hated Jacob because of the blessing wherewith his father blessed him: and Esau said in his heart, The days of mourning for

my father are at hand; then I will slay my brother Jacob"
(Genesis 27:41).

## Esau's Hatred Persists

The Old Testament command is, "Thou shalt not hate thy
brother in thy heart" (Leviticus 19:17). The New Testament
informs us that he who hates is a murderer. In I John 3:15,
we read, "Whosoever hateth his brother is a murderer, and ye
know that no murderer has eternal life dwelling in him."
Then in I John 2:9, there is this word, "He that saith he is
in the light and hateth his brother is in the darkness even
until now."

The virus of Esau's hatred was passed from one generation
to the next. Nor did his descendants ever lose the spirit of
murder. They even gloried in the slaughter of Jacob's descendants.

Learning of Esau's plan to kill him, Jacob fled to the home
of his mother's brother in Padan-Aram. Esau then journeyed
south of the Dead Sea to the land of Seir, the country of Edom.

Years later Esau and Jacob meet for the last time. Jacob,
now called Israel, is returning with his wives, his children,
his flocks, and herds to Canaan. It is a fearful experience for
him. He knows that unless the Lord protects him, he will
lose his life by Esau's sword. But the Lord protects him and
for one fleeting hour, Jacob and Esau exchange greetings and
then go their separate ways, never to meet again.

"So Esau returned that day on his way unto Seir" (Genesis
33:16). These are almost the last words we read of Esau in
the Old Testament. But they are not the last words we read of
his descendants. They became the bitterest and most implacable enemies of Israel. They lived by the sword and they had
no greater delight than to witness the persecution of God's
people and the destruction of their holy places. It is against
such a nation that Obadiah pronounces God's judgment.

Petrie is right when he suggests that Edom (red) was
well named. He says, "The scarlet line runs through Edom
the nation, Edom the country, and Edom the destiny. Edom's
history is written in crimson letters; the history of blood. By
the bloody sword the Edomites captured Mount Seir from
the Horites. By the sword, they battled with Israel. By the

sword, they won southern Palestine. By the sword, they performed the last act in their long historic drama."

Men who live by the sword also perish by the sword. Those who destroy are destroyed. And Obadiah prophetically records the awful totality of Edom's destruction. God will not be mocked, for though the wicked temporarily prosper, judgment is ever near. And whatsoever a man (or nation) sows, that shall he also reap. Obadiah strongly believed in the "indestructable character of eternal justice."

# Chapter III

## IDENTIFYING AND DATING OBADIAH

### *Who Was Obadiah?*

It is an important part of Biblical research to identify the author and to date his writing. With many of the Scripture writers this is easily done. But not so with Obadiah. There are not less than twelve Obadiahs in the Old Testament. Not one of them can be authoritatively identified with the author of this prophecy.

Josephus, however, tries to relate the author of this little prophetic book with the governor of Ahab's household.

> "And it came to pass after many days, that the word of the Lord came to Elijah in the third year, saying, Go, show thyself unto Ahab; and I will send rain upon the earth. And Elijah went to show himself unto Ahab. And there was a sore famine in Samaria. And Ahab called Obadiah, which was the governor of his house. (Now Obadiah feared the Lord greatly: For it was so, when Jezebel cut off the prophets of the Lord, that Obadiah took an hundred prophets, and hid them by fifty in a cave, and fed them with bread and water)" (I Kings 18: 1-4).

Though it would be nice to have the assurance that wicked Ahab's good governor was the author of Obadiah, yet most Bible commentators agree with Matthew Henry that "we have no proof" for such an assumption.

Others claim the author of this twenty-one verse book is one of the princes of Judah who lived in the days of Jehoshaphat. Those princes played a significant part in the spiritual awakening which took place under the rule of Jehoshaphat.

> "Also in the third year of his reign he sent to his princes, even to Ben-hail, and to Obadiah, and to Zechariah, and

to Nethaneel, and to Michaiah, to teach in the cities of Judah" (II Chronicles 17:7).

Some commentators point to the brave Gadite leader who joined David during those years in which Saul was his bitter enemy.

"And of the Gadites there separated themselves unto David into the hold to the wilderness men of might, and men of war fit for the battle, that could handle shield and buckler, whose faces were like the faces of lions, and were as swift as the roes upon the mountains; Ezer the first, Obadiah the second, Eliab the third" (I Chronicles 12: 8, 9).

Others relate Obadiah to the repairing of the temple in Jerusalem during the reign of Josiah.

"And the men did the work faithfully: and the overseers of them were Jahath and Obadiah, the Levites, of the sons of Merari; and Zechariah and Meshullam, of the sons of the Kohathites, to set it forward; and other of the Levites, all that could skill of instruments of music" (II Chronicles 34:12).

All of this, however, is guesswork and lacks the stamp of authority. We are left, therefore, to assume that the identification of the author would not necessarily serve any significant purpose. The author himself was more concerned about getting his message across than about revealing his identity. The Spirit of the Lord was apparently pleased to concur with Obadiah in this.

### When Did Obadiah Write?

If it is difficult to identify the author, it is more difficult to state with assurance the time of his writing. Commentators leave us with a wide division of opinion in this regard.

The key to the dating of the book seems to be found in the interpretation one gives to verses 11-14:

"In the day that thou stoodest on the other side, in the day that the strangers carried away captive his forces, and foreigners entered into his gates, and cast lots upon

Jerusalem, even thou wast as one of them. But thou shouldest not have looked on the day of thy brother in the day that he became a stranger; neither shouldest thou have rejoiced over the children of Judah in the day of their destruction; neither shouldest thou have spoken proudly in the day of distress. Thou shouldest not have entered into the gate of my people in the day of their calamity; yea, thou shouldest not have looked on their affliction in the day of their calamity, nor have laid hands on their substance in the day of their calamity; Neither shouldest thou have stood in the crossway, to cut off those of his that did escape; neither shouldest thou have delivered up those of his that did remain in the day of distress."

The difficulty in interpreting this passage arises from the fact that the event described apparently can fit into any of several places in Israel's history.

### Jerusalem Overrun

Jerusalem was sacked by her enemies on numerous occasions. She was first overrun by Shishak, king of Egypt, during the fifth year of the reign of King Rehoboam.

"And he took away the treasures of the house of the Lord, and the treasures of the king's house; he even took away all: and he took away all the shields of gold which Solomon had made" (I Kings 14:26).

We learn, however, from II Chronicles 12 that through the intervention of the prophet Shemaiah the king and princes of Israel were led to humble themselves. The Lord then granted them deliverance. This event does not appear, therefore, to fully fit the picture given by Obadiah.

II Chronicles 21 tells us of a second occasion in which Jerusalem was overrun. Jehoram, son of Jehoshaphat, was ruling in Jerusalem. He revolted against the godly example of his father and did that which was evil in the eyes of the Lord. In the light of this, the Edomites who were at that time under the dominion of Judah, revolted against Jehoram. Elijah then forewarned King Jehoram that the judgment of God

27

would come upon Judah in the form of a great plague and sickness.

"Moreover the Lord stirred up against Jehoram the spirit of the Philistines, and of the Arabians, that were near the Ethiopians: And they came up into Judah, and brake into it, and carried away all the substance that was found in the king's house, and his sons also, and his wives; so that there was never a son left him, save Jehoahaz, the youngest of his sons" (II Chronicles 21:16, 17).

Though these were tragic days in Jerusalem, they too seem to fall short of the events described by Obadiah.

The third occasion in which Judah was sacked is recorded in II Kings 8:14 and II Chronicles 25:17-24. In these passages, we discover that Amaziah, king of Judah, smote ten thousand Edomites and took ten thousand more captives. The tragedy is that, after the victory, the king took the gods of the "children of Seir" (Edomites) and "set them up to be his gods, and bowed down himself before them, and burned incense unto them" (II Chronicles 25:14). Then in the pride of his heart, King Amaziah felt he was prepared to do battle against Joash, king of Israel. But God delivered Amaziah into the hands of the armies of Israel because Judah had sought after the gods of Edom.

"And Judah was put to the worse before Israel, and they fled every man to his tent. And Joash the king of Israel took Amaziah king of Judah, the son of Joash, the son of Jehohaz, at Beth-shemesh, and brought him to Jerusalem, and brake down the wall of Jerusalem from the gate of Ephraim to the corner gate, four hundred cubits. And he took all the gold and the silver, and all the vessels that were found in the house of God with Obed-edom, and the treasures of the king's house, the hostages also, and returned to Samaria" (II Chronicles 25:22-24).

Though this historical account probably comes closer to paralleling the experience described by Obadiah, yet there are too many details lacking to enable one to say with assurance that it is the same event.

Let us look, therefore, at another time in which Jerusalem was sacked. The account is found in II Kings 25. It records

the destruction of Jerusalem by the Chaldean king Nebuchadnezzar. The seige of Jerusalem and the utter destruction of
it is a dreadful story of death, bloodshed, and devastation.
The walls of the city were torn down. Thousands of inhabitants were slaughtered. The house of the Lord was burned to
the ground and the gold, silver, and brass carried to Babylon.

The almost total destruction of Jerusalem and its populace
described in II Kings 25 appears to many commentators to
be that to which Obadiah refers in his prophecy. However, we
cannot be dogmatic. Biblical scholars cannot agree that *any*
of the above-mentioned events can be pinpointed definitely
as the one to which Obadiah refers.

### Placing Obadiah before Nebuchadnezzar

G. Campbell Morgan in his book, *The Minor Prophets*, states
categorically that it is impossible to fix the date of the Obadiah
prophecy accurately. He seems, however, to favor the view
that the prophecy was written before the Babylonian capture
of Jerusalem.

Morgan agrees with the Biblical revisors that the tense of
the verb translated in the King James, "thou shouldest not have
looked . . ." should read, "look not," or "you should not
look." He feels the imperative form of the verb should be used
in verses 12, 13 and 14. The prophecy then becomes a warning to the Edomites with respect to their behavior in a forth-
coming event.

Furthermore, Morgan believes Obadiah borrows from both
Joel and Amos. He feels Obadiah's statement, "For the day of
the Lord is near upon all the heathen," has been borrowed
from Joel's statement in 1:15, "Alas, for the day! for the day
of the Lord is at hand." He is convinced that when Obadiah
states, "Upon Mount Zion shall be deliverance and there shall
be holiness; and the house of Jacob shall possess their possessions," he has borrowed from Joel 3:17: "So shall ye know
that I am the Lord your God dwelling in Zion, my holy mountain: then shall Jerusalem behold me and there shall no strangers pass through her any more."

It is Morgan's conviction that Obadiah's statement found in
verse 19: "And they of the south shall possess the mount of
Esau; and they of the plain the Philistines: and they shall

possess the fields of Ephraim, and the fields of Samaria; and Benjamin shall possess Gilead," has been borrowed from Amos 9:12: "That they may possess the remnant of Edom, and of all the heathen, which are called by my name, saith the Lord that doeth this."

Though this view places the prophecy of Obadiah after the writings of Joel and Amos, it allows for the book to be written before the Babylonian captivity.

Matthew Henry agrees that Obadiah may have been contemporary with Joel and Amos. This places him around 800 B.C. and would mean he could not have been an eyewitness to the Babylonian destruction of Jerusalem. If this is true, then that portion of the prophecy which appears to be historical rather than prophetic (vv. 11-14) was given to Obadiah by the eternal Spirit of the Lord to whom future history is ever contemporary.

The *Self-Interpreting Bible* concurs with Matthew Henry that Obadiah was probably a contemporary of Joel. The suggestion is that he wrote before Jeremiah and did not witness the Babylonian captivity. He did, however, know about the sack of Jerusalem in the reign of Jehoram.

Sampey's *Syllabus of Old Testament Study* places Obadiah at 800 B.C., thereby making him one of the earliest of the writing prophets. Such a view stands in bold contrast to Lange and several other commentators who believe Obadiah prophesied after the destruction of Jerusalem by Nebuchadnezzar.

## Dating Obadiah after Nebuchadnezzar

The *New Bible Commentary* claims Obadiah prophesied after the Babylonian destruction of Jerusalem. The authors of the *Wycliffe Bible Commentator* agree with this position and, therefore, place the writing of Obadiah's book sometime after 586 B.C.

J. L. Eason is convinced Obadiah must have either seen or known of the destruction of Jerusalem carried out by Nebuchadnezzar in 586 B.C. and dates the writing of Obadiah after the destruction.

## Bible Survey

F. W. Farrar in his book, *The Minor Prophets,* says there is "a high degree of probability that Obadiah wrote shortly after the final invasion of Nebuchadnezzar." He is certain Obadiah must have written after the dispersion of the northern kingdom because there is no mention of the northern kingdom tribes.

J. P. Lewis in his book, *The Minor Prophets*, says the commentators set dates for the authorship of Obadiah anywhere from 850 B.C. to 312 B.C. Lewis himself claims that "despite all cases made, the calamity spoken of in verses 11-14 can hardly be other than that brought about by Nebuchadnezzar in 586 B.C."

## A Middle Ground

Between the opposing positions of early and late authorship is a middle ground held by Laetsch. He accepts neither the 800 B.C. date nor the post-captivity date. It is his strong conviction that Obadiah 11-14 does not describe Nebuchadnezzar's sack of Jerusalem.

Laetsch says, "In spite of the confident assertions of many writers, we hold that Obadiah is not speaking of the destruction in 586 B.C.; neither prophetically or retrospectively." He argues that though Obadiah enumerates a number of harrowing details of the great calamity, he does not mention the six characteristic marks of 586 B.C.:

(1) The razing of the walls of Jerusalem (II Kings 25: 10; Jeremiah 52:14; Nehemiah 2:13-17).

(2) The burning of the royal palace and houses (II Kings 25:9; Jeremiah 52:13).

(3) The burning of the temple (II Kings 25:9; Jeremiah 52:13).

(4) The capture and deportation to Babylon of the king (II Kings 25:7).

(5) The deportation to Babylon of the entire nation with a few exceptions (II Kings 25:11).

(6) The immigration of the Jews to Egypt (II Kings 25: 26; Jeremiah 41:6; 43:22).

"Moreover," says Laetsch, "the Authorized Version rendering of verses 12-14, 'Thou shouldest not have,' is not only contrary to the Hebrew grammar . . . it is also strange to say the least, to warn a nation against a sin long past. To regard the last clause of verse 11 as prophetic, 'Thou shalt be as one of them,' asserting a future fact, and then warning against that very fact in order to prevent its accomplishment, is utterly illogical. God never speaks in that manner. Neither the prophetic or retrospective interpretation is acceptable in view of the actual situation it is to describe."

Laetsch is convinced the solution to the problem is "to regard the prophet as an eyewitness of a calamitous destruction of Jerusalem." He feels this was the destruction which took place during the reign of Jehoram. It was at this time that the "Philistines and Arabian tribes from southern Arabia attacked Judah, destroyed Jerusalem, pillaged the royal palace and the city and took Jehoram's wives and children captive."

"Here," says Laetsch, "we have an historical situation which exactly fits the calamity which Obadiah describes. Hence, the dating of this book in the time of Jehoram is in full keeping with Biblical facts, with grammar and logic."

Because of this wide divergence of opinion concerning the date of the prophecy, it may prove wise for the reader to accept John Calvin's attitude. He says, "I know not whether Obadiah and Jeremiah are contemporaries, and on this subject we need not so much labor. It is sufficient for us to know, that this prophecy was added to other prophecies, that the Israelites might feel assured, that through their kindred the Idumeans might prosper for a time, yet they could not escape the hand of God, but would shortly be constrained to give an account of their cruelty, inasmuch as they had without cause been all aflame against the distressed and afflicted people of God" (*Calvin's Commentaries — Minor Prophets*, Vol. II).

We may be assured that the Holy Spirit made no mistake in not dating the book for us. Obadiah's message is obviously more important than the date of his writing. Let the concern of the reader, therefore, coincide with the concern of the writer so that the impact of the message may reach his heart. Though we cannot date the book nor identify the human author, we can receive the message God has for us, and this is basic to all profitable Bible study.

# Chapter IV

## LOCATING THE EDOMITES

One of the last Old Testament pictures we see of Esau the father of the Edomites is drawn for us in Genesis 33:16, where we read: "So Esau returned that day on his way unto Seir." Then in Genesis 36:1, we are introduced to the descendants of Esau: "Now these are the generations of Esau, who is Edom." The close relationship between Esau, Edom, and Mount Seir is pointed up in the eighth and ninth verses of this same chapter: "Thus dwelled Esau in Mount Seir: Esau is Edom. And these are the generations of Esau, the father of the Edomites in Mount Seir."

The land of Edom (Mount Seir) is a mountainous territory covering about three thousand square miles. It is a narrow stretch of land running approximately one hundred miles north and south by thirty miles east and west. It is bounded on the north by the southern shores of the Dead Sea and on the south by the Gulf of Aqaba. It encompasses a part of the Wilderness of Zin. Though much of the territory is barren and precipitous, it is not without some fertile valleys.

Its main city in the north was Bozrah, which was an almost impregnable fortress. Farther south was the city of Temen which was protected by the fortress of Petra (identified in the Bible as Sela).

### Petra the Beautiful

The pride and self-confidence of the Edomites can be understood as one understands the location of their fortress at Petra. A Swiss traveler by the name of John Lewis Burckhardt went to the city of Petra in 1812. Because the city was considered sacred by the Arabs and because they would be apt to kill any infidel who set foot therein, it was necessary for Burckhardt to disguise himself as a Bedouin sheikh. Widespread interest in the city was later aroused as the result of Burckhardt's report of what he had seen.

"For situation and natural beauty," says G. L. Robinson, "Petra is unique among the cities of the earth. To describe it adequately is an impossibility. Its location, deep down among the mountains of Seir, surrounded on all sides by richly colored rocks of simply matchless beauty and grandeur, renders it a wonder of the desert.

"One enters the weird but attractive city by a narrow gorge a mile long. This defile is one of the most magnificent and romantic avenues of its kind in all nature. A tiny stream flows under one's feet much of the way. The chasm is both narrow and deep, ofttimes so contracted as to be almost dark at noonday. The rocks which bound it are tinted most beautifully with all the colors of the rainbow. On emerging from it into the great hollow basin which is over a mile long by two-thirds of a mile broad, the explorer is confronted by rock-hewn dwellings, temples, and other cuttings on every side. Several hundred of these still remain all carved literally out of the solid sandstone rock. The ruins of the castle still stand scattered over the bottom of the city's site. The colors of the rocks add immensely to the attractiveness of the place. The deepest reds, purple, orange, yellow, white, violet, and other colors are arranged by nature in ordered bands, shading off artistically into one another.

"The entire city and its environs are one immense maze of richly colored mountains and clifts, chasms and rocky shelves and narrow valleys, gorges and plateaus, shady dells and sunny promontories, grand and beautiful, just the ideal of beauty and protection for a fortress of trade and commerce to satisfy an oriental nomad. But, alas! desolation now reigns within and about it on every hand, and Obadiah's warnings and predictions have been woefully verified!" — *The Twelve Minor Prophets*

In the *National Geographic* of February, 1935, there appeared an article on the city of Petra written by John D. Whiting. In it this information is included:

"Petra, silent city of the forgotten past, halfway between the Dead Sea and the Gulf of Aqaba, exerts a magic spell upon the minds of those fortunate enough to know it. Its single and weird approach, through a deep rock cleft more than a mile long; its temples, numbering near a thousand, cut into the living rock of the stupendous clifts showing Babylonian, Egyptian, Greek, and Roman influence; its high places, courts, libations, and altars where the ancients worshipped; its amazing color, work of nature lavish with ochar and all shades of red — all these are mysterious, enthralling.

"For centuries, Petra was a rich caravan city, a veritable crossroads of the ancient world. Treasures were brought to Petra for storage and for transshipment in every direction. So important was the city that the Romans built two roads to tap its wealth. When Rome fell, however, its doom was sealed."

Joseph Hoffman Cohn of the American Board of Missions to the Jews refers to Petra as "the rose red city, half as old as time," and says that it once had a population of 267,000 people.

### The Biblical Picture

It will be recalled by the reader that the children of Israel were commanded by God not to hate the Edomites. "Thou shalt not abhor an Edomite; for he is thy brother . . ." (Deuteronomy 23:7). It may also be recalled that the children of Israel requested permission to pass through the territory of Mount Seir when they returned from Egypt but it was denied them.

"And Moses sent messengers from Kadesh unto the king of Edom, Thus saith thy brother Israel, Thou knowest all the travail that hath befallen us: How our fathers went down into Egypt, and we have dwelt in Egypt a long time; and the Egyptians vexed us, and our fathers: And when we cried unto the Lord, he heard our voice, and sent an angel, and hath brought us forth out of Egypt: and, behold, we are in Kadesh, a city in the uttermost of thy border: Let us pass, I pray thee, through thy country: we will not pass through the fields, or through the vineyards, neither will we drink of the water of the wells: we will go by the king's high way, we will not turn to the right hand nor to the left, until we have passed thy borders. And Edom said unto him, Thou shalt not pass by me, lest I come out against thee with the sword. And the children of Israel said unto him, We will go by the high way: and if I and my cattle drink of thy water, then I will pay for it: I will only, without doing any thing else, go through on my feet. And he said, Thou shalt not go through. And Edom came out against him with much people and with a strong hand. Thus Edom refused to give Israel passage through his border: wherefore Israel turned away from him" (Numbers 20:14-21).

This, of course, increased the animosity between the two nations. And all through Old Testament history we find sporadic fighting between the descendants of Esau and the descendants of Jacob.

In I Samuel 14, we are told that when Saul became the king of Israel, he fought against his enemies on every side including the Edomites and delivered Israel out of the hands of them that spoiled them. Later on in II Samuel 8, we discover that David raised up a garrison throughout all of Edom and the Edomites became David's servants.

However, when Solomon became king, the picture changed. The sad story is given to us in I Kings:

"And the Lord stirred up an adversary unto Solomon, Hadad the Edomite: he was of the king's seed in Edom. For it came to pass, when David was in Edom, and Joab the captain of the host was gone up to bury the slain, after he had smitten every male in Edom; (For six months did Joab remain there with all Israel, until he had cut off every male in Edom:) That Hadad fled, he and certain Edomites of his father's servants with him, to go into Egypt; Hadad being yet a little child. And they arose out of Midian, and came to Paran: and they took men with them out of Paran, and they came to Egypt, unto Pharoah king of Egypt; which gave him an house, and appointed him victuals, and gave him land. And Hadad found great favor in the sight of Pharoah, so that he gave him to wife the sister of his own wife, the sister of Tahpenes the queen. And the sister of Tahpenes bare him Genubath his son, whom Tahpenes weaned in Pharoah's house: and Genubath was in Pharoah's household among the sons of Pharoah. And when Hadad heard in Egypt that David slept with his fathers, and that Joab the captain of the host was dead, Hadad said to Pharoah, Let me depart, that I may go to mine own country. Then Pharoah said unto him, But what hast thou lacked with me, that, behold, thou seekest to go to thine own country? And he answered, Nothing: howbeit let me go in any wise. And God stirred him up another adversary, Rezon the son of Eliadah, which fled from his lord Hadadezer king of Zobah: And he gathered men unto him, and became captain over a band, when David slew them of Zobah: and they went to Damascus, and dwelt therein, and reigned in Damascus. And he was an adversary to Israel all the days of Solomon, beside the mischief that Hadad did: and he abhorred Israel, and reigned over Syria" (I Kings 11:14-25).

Conflicts between the Israelites and the Edomites continued to the time of the Babylonian captivity, at which time the descendants of Esau rose up against the already defeated descendants of Jacob. This background helps to clarify the purpose for Obadiah's prophecy.

## Chapter V

# THE MESSAGE OF OBADIAH

### The Certainty of Judgment

*"The vision of Obadiah. Thus saith the Lord God concerning Edom; We have heard a rumor from the Lord, and an ambassador is sent among the heathen, Arise ye, and let us rise up against her in battle" (Obadiah 1).*

At the outset of his message, Obadiah states that what he has to declare he has received from the Lord. The vision he is revealing has been given him of God — God is the author. His message carries with it the authoritative weight of "Thus saith the Lord God."

"What Obadiah wrote was not the product of his own reflection, his keen insight into the political and religious conditions of his day, nor was it merely the application of God's Word to a given situation. It was a vision, a divine revelation of God's promise" (*The Minor Prophets*, T. Laetsch).

In this, Obadiah's attitude is characteristic of all Old and New Testament writers. They wrote with a deep conviction that their message was not their own. They shared with others that which God first spoke to them. This accounts for the holy boldness with which the prophets spoke and wrote. They were holy men of God, recording and declaring God's message.

Obadiah is not the only Old Testament prophet to use the term, "a vision." Daniel, Isaiah, Jeremiah, Ezekiel, Zechariah and others refer to having received visions from the Lord. In some cases, the visions were audio-visual (an appearance of the angel of the Lord) and in other cases they were only audio but seen in the sense that they were perceived by the ear.

The word "rumor" is better translated "tidings," or "report," and the word, "heathen," as "nations." The verse could more freely read, "We have heard a report from the Lord that He has sent ambassadors among the nations, crying, Alert your armies and send them into battle against Edom."

"We might think of the ambassadors of some human king who was sending them to some surrounding kingdoms, urging them to join in a campaign against Edom. It may, however, be preferable to regard the ambassadors in the light of I Kings 32:19-38, where the Lord, in order to destroy Ahab, sent a lying spirit, who through the prophets, promised success to Ahab's campaign. So the Lord now sends His spirits who through the ambassadors persuade the nations to join in a united attack upon Edom. The conspiring nations, of course, had their own ambitious interests in mind, but unknown to themselves, they were only pawns in the hands of the Lord. It is the Lord who places Himself at the head of this undertaking" (Laetsch).

Obadiah, verse 1, introduces us to the sovereignty of God. It suggests that God rules in the kingdom of men. He both raises up nations and sets them down according to His own purposes.

"God is behind those scenes of conflict which appear to be natural uprisings. The wars and rumors of wars which break out between apparently friendly nations or allies are related to the sovereign will of God in accomplishing His work."

Wise is the man who discerns the hand of God moving earthly kingdoms. His heart will not fail for fear when nations rise and fall.

The Old Testament has certainly been written for our instruction in this regard. Even a sketchy knowledge of the Egyptian, Babylonian, Medio-Persian, Greek and Roman empires gives credence to this. While the biographies of such empire-influencing characters as Moses, Joseph, Daniel, and Queen Esther strengthen one's faith in this matter.

"Wars are not stirred up at random," says Calvin, "but by the secret influence of God; as though He said, 'When tumult arises, let us not think that its beginning is from the earth, but that God Himself is the mover.' "

Though there are many prophetic statements in the Bible which relate to the Gentile nations as a whole, there are also prophetic statements which point the finger at a specific nation or people. In this case, Obadiah informs us that God's message specifically concerns the nation of Edom. We have already learned that the Edomites were descendants of Esau and that they lived in an area southeast of Israel.

*"Behold, I have made thee small among the heathen: thou art greatly despised"* (*Obadiah* 2).

In *Living Prophecies*, the verse reads, "I will cut you down to size among the nations, Edom, making you small and despised."

What a clear statement of God's planned judgment against Edom this is. And the implication is intrinsic within the statement that God can do what He declares He will do.

Laetsch in his commentary on *The Minor Prophets* says, "The Lord is sure of the success of His plans. He already sees Edom shorn of all the power and glory, covered with contempt and shame, although the enemies are still preparing their plans."

The Eternal God with whom there is no past, present, or future, sees future events as though they were already accomplished. In some cases, these events are prophetically reported. This is illustrated in the verb tenses used in the phrases, "I have made thee small . . . Thou art greatly despised."

This reminds us of our Lord's condemnation of those cities, "wherein most of His mighty works were done." He singled out Capernaum, for special judgment as He said, "And thou Capernaum, which art exalted unto heaven, shall be brought down to hell; for if the mighty works, which have been done in thee, had been done in Sodom, it would have remained until this day. But I say unto you, that it shall be more tolerable for the land of Sodom in the day of judgment than for thee" (Matthew 11:23, 24). History has long since testified to the fulfillment of this judgment against Capernaum.

At the very time in which Edom appeared to be powerful and well favored among the nations, she was already marked out for destruction. How big she looked to the Israelites. How small she looked to Him before whom the nations are as the small dust in a balance. Obviously, we need to learn to look upon the wealth and might of men and nations with God-given perspective.

*"The pride of thine heart hath deceived thee, thou that dwellest in the clefts of the rock, whose habitation is high; that saith in his heart, Who shall bring me down to the ground? Though thou exalt thyself as the eagle, and though thou set thy nest among the stars, thence will I bring thee down, saith the Lord"* (*Obadiah 3, 4*).

"The prophet names four items on which the pride of Edom was based: its power, its wealth, its alliances, its wisdom. But not one of these advantages or all of them combined could prevent its ignominious ruin," says Calvin.

While the Israelites were in a sad and down-trodden condition, the Edomites felt overwhelmingly secure because of their military alliances and their geographic location. Self-confidence had overcome them and pride had filled their hearts. These sons of Esau desperately needed to hear the voice of the writer of the Proverbs, "A man's pride shall bring him low" (29:23). "Pride goeth before destruction, and a haughty spirit before a fall" (16:18). "Seest thou a man wise in his own conceit? There is more hope of a fool than of him" (26:12).

Through Isaiah God pronounces His severest judgments against the proud of heart:

"For the day of the Lord of hosts shall be upon everyone that is proud and lofty, and upon everyone that is lifted up; and he shall be brought low" (2:12).

One is reminded that pride was at the heart of Satan's fall.

"For thou hast said in thine heart, I will ascend into heaven, I will exalt my throne above the stars of God: I will sit also upon the mount of the congregation, in the sides of the north: I will ascend above the heights of the clouds; I will be like the most High" (Isaiah 14: 13, 14).

God's response to such arrogancy was,

"Thou shalt be brought down to hell, to the sides of the pit" (Isaiah 14:15).

In Ezekiel 28, the prophet addresses a message of the Lord to the prince of Tyrus. He says,

"Thus saith the Lord God; Because thine heart is lifted up, and thou hast said, I am a God, I sit in the seat of God, in the midst of the seas; yet thou art a man, and not God, though thou set thine heart as the heart of God" (28:2).

God's reaction to such pride is,

"Behold, therefore I will bring strangers upon thee, the terrible of the nations: and they shall draw their swords against the beauty of thy wisdom, and they shall defile thy brightness. They shall bring thee down to the pit, and thou shalt die the deaths of them that are slain in the midst of the seas. Wilt thou yet say before him that slayeth thee, I am God? but thou shalt be a man, and no God, in the hand of him that slayeth thee. Thou shalt die the deaths of the uncircumcised by the hand of strangers: for I have spoken it, saith the Lord God" (Ezekiel 28:7-10).

Amos says concerning the proud, "Though they dig into hell, thence shall mine hand take them; though they climb up to heaven, thence will I bring them down" (9:2). Habakkuk adds, "Woe to him that coveteth an evil covetousness to his house, that he may set his nest on high, that he may be delivered from the power of evil!" (2:9).

How greatly the Lord humbled the hardened heart of Pharoah with judgment after judgment. And in the end, this proud ruler and his chariots were cast into the sea.

The blasphemous Sennacherib, king of the Assyrians, defied God to deliver Israel out of his hand. The situation looked utterly hopeless for Israel but God had the last word.

"And the Lord sent an angel which cut off all the mighty men of valor, and the leaders and the captains in the camp of the king of Assyria. So he returned with shame of face to his own land. And when he was come into the house of his god, they that came forth of his own bowels slew him there with the sword" (II Chronicles 32:21).

For added assurance that God knows how to humble the proud, read the account of His dealings with Nebuchadnezzar in Daniel 4. Then follow through with the humbling of king Belshazzar in Daniel 5.

And who could have been of prouder heart than Haman, prime minister of the great King Ahasuerus. How arrogantly he told his friends of "the glory of his riches, and the multitude of his children, and all the things wherein the king had promoted him, and how he had advanced him above the princes and servants of the king" (Esther 5:11). But Haman's cup of pride could not be filled to the full until he could hang Mordecai upon the gallows. And how does this story of obnoxious self-aggrandizement end? "So they hanged Haman on the gallows that he had prepared for Mordecai" (Esther 7:10).

With all of this as background, it is little wonder the New Testament has so much to say about humility. There should be no room for any "I-thank-thee-that-I-am-not-as-other-men" attitude in the heart of the child of God. The Christian's initial approach to God is on the basis of "God be merciful to me, a sinner." His continued fellowship with God is based on walking in humility.

It would be well for us who are so easily tempted to yield to the pride of life to give heed to the warning of Revelation 3:17, 18:

"Because thou sayest, I am rich, and increased with goods, and have need of nothing; and knowest not that thou art wretched, and miserable, and poor, and blind, and naked: I counsel thee to buy of me gold tried in the fire, that thou mayest be rich; and white raiment, that thou mayest be clothed, and that the shame of thy nakedness do not appear; and anoint thine eyes with eyesalve, that thou mayest see."

God does indeed know how to humble the proud though they exalt themselves as the eagle, and though they build their nests among the stars.

In these days of advanced science in which men and nations talk much about interplanetary travel and space stations, we need to beware as nations lest we exalt ourselves out of proportion. We need to take careful heed lest we follow in the footsteps of him who was the father of lies and who would deceive us through the pride of our hearts.

These are days in which men are making attempts to dethrone God. They will highly exalt themselves through great wonders and miracles and will claim to be God. They will deceive many causing them to bow the knee before the false prophet and the anti-Christ.

General Omar Bradley has said that we are living in a day in which "We have too many men of science, and too few men of God. We have grasped the mystery of the atom, and rejected the Sermon on the Mount. The world has achieved brilliance without wisdom, power without conscience. Ours is a world of nuclear giants and ethical infants."

We are warned in II Thessalonians 2 that there is a day ahead in which there will be a great falling away from and rebellion against God. And then the man of sin, the son of perdition, will be revealed. He will exalt himself above all that is called God or that is worshipped so "that he as god sitteth in the temple of God showing himself that he is god." However, even this proud and wicked one shall be humbled for the Lord will consume him with the breath of His mouth and destroy him by His very presence.

God's fierce judgment on Edom's pride should say something to all of us.

> *"If thieves came to thee, if robbers by night (how art thou cut off!) would they not have stolen till they had enough? if the grapegatherers came to thee, would they not leave some grapes? How are the things of Esau searched out! how are his hidden things sought up! (Obadiah 5, 6).*

The Edomites had much wealth to be coveted by others. Not all of Edom was desert land. She possessed some fertile valleys which were well watered both by rain and irrigation. But what was perhaps most important to her was her location. Her chief cities controlled the great trade routes from Ezion-Geber, one leading to Egypt, the other running from the port through the length of Edom and Transjordania north to Damascus. She traded wares with Arabia, India, Africa, Egypt, Syria, and Assyria. She "served as the conqueror of this worldwide trade, exacting duties, tolls, and other taxes, buying and selling at great profit." Furthermore, "the rich copper and iron mines of Ezion-Geber were a source of great wealth."

But note the awful extent to which the plundering and destruction of Edom would be carried out. The implication is that the Edomites would be far better off if their homes were overrun by thieves and their vineyards by grapegatherers. At least thieves would take only the things they want and leave much behind. The grapegatherers would take only that which they could carry and the gleanings would be left. But in the judgment that was to fall upon Edom, "every nook and cranny will be searched and robbed and every treasure found out and taken" (Obadiah 6, *Living Prophecies*).

"We hence learn that as men in vain seek hiding places for themselves that they may be safe from dangers; so in vain they conceal their riches; for the hand of God can penetrate into the depths of the sea, and to the heights of the heavens. Nothing then remains for us but ever to offer ourselves and all our things to God. He protects us under His wings, we shall be safe in the midst of them from all dangers; but if we think that subterfuges will be of any avail to us, we deceive ourselves" (Calvin).

It is a fearful thing to fall into the hands of the living God. There is no judgment as complete and as final as that which He ministers. God is a consuming fire. This is not to suggest that God is not merciful and long-suffering. The Bible is filled with multiplied evidences of His mercy. But when He acts in judgment, it is utterly devastating.

Both the mercy and wrath of God are vividly pictured for us in the destruction of Sodom and Gomorrah. The stench of Sodom's sin was abhorrent to the nostrils of almighty God. And yet He was willing to listen to the intercession of Abraham in behalf of that wicked city. He was prepared to spare the city from judgment if but ten righteous were found therein. But when even Lot's sons-in-law mocked at the impending judgment, the Lord rained fire and brimstone from heaven upon the city and destroyed it.

As God loves with an infinite love, so He hates with a perfect hatred. Both His goodness and His wrath are meant to turn men to repentance. When His mercy is rejected, His anger is suffered.

While many of the cities of Palestine have remained inhabited through the centuries, Petra and the other fortress cities of the Edomites have long since been little more than

45

hunting grounds for the archaeologists and nesting places for birds and reptiles.

> "All the men of thy confederacy have brought thee even to the border: the men that were at peace with thee have deceived thee, and prevailed against thee; they that eat thy bread have laid a wound under thee: there is none understanding in him" (Obadiah 7).

Because of Edom's great wealth and power, it was not difficult for her to make alliances with neighboring states. She succeeded in making "trade pacts, defense agreements, and other covenants with not a few nations."

But Edom's allies were to become her undoing. She had made her covenants without taking God into consideration. They who ate bread with her would become her enemies. This reminds us of another case in religious history where a "friend" ate bread with Another only to lift up his heel against Him and betray Him.

Oh, the frailty of human alliances. The prophet states that Edom's allies would turn against her. While they are promising her peace, they are actually plotting her destruction. Furthermore, their behavior is instigated by the Lord of Hosts. He is behind the scenes, manipulating this plot against the Edomites.

History is replete with illustrations of friends becoming enemies almost overnight. This is true not only on the individual level but also on the national and international level. Note the civil wars of history where brothers have fought brothers. Think of the international peace treaties that have been signed simply to buy time so one "friend" could better prepare to attack another.

"The prophet upbraids the Idumeans, and says, that their confederates and friends would prove their ruin, because they had conspired among themselves beyond what was just and right. When men thus mutually join together, there are none of them who do not greedily seek their own vantage; in the meantime, both sides are deceived; but God disconcerts their counsel, and blasts the issue, because they regard not their end. And when the wicked seek friendships, they plot something that is wrong; they either try to injure the innocent, or they seek some advantage. All the compacts then which the ungodly and despisers of God make with one another, have always something vicious intermixed; and it is, therefore, no wonder that the Lord disappoints them of their hope, and curses their counsels" (Calvin).

> "*Shall I not in that day, saith the Lord, even destroy the wise men out of Edom, and understanding out of the mount of Esau?*" (*Obadiah* 8).

The term "mount of Esau" is synonymous with Edom. It is used again in verses 19 and 21. "Mount of Esau" stands in contrast to "Mount Zion." The subject will be dealt with further in the comments made on verse 19.

"The wise men of Edom and the cleverness of Mount Esau were notorious. It is the race which has given to history the Herods . . . clever, scheming, ruthless statesmen, as able as they were false and bitter, as shrewd in policy as they were destitute of ideals. 'That fox,' cried Christ, and crying stamped the race" (G. A. Smith).

The Lord vowed to destroy the wise out of Edom and understanding out of the mount of Esau. It must be remembered that it was the God of all wisdom speaking. Before Him, the wisdom of men is foolishness. In I Corinthians, we read:

> "For it is written, I will destroy the wisdom of the wise, and will bring to nothing the understanding of the prudent. Where is the wise? where is the scribe? where is the disputer of this world? hath not God made foolish the wisdom of this world? For after that in the wisdom of God the world by wisdom knew not God, it pleased God by the foolishness of preaching to save them that believe. For the Jews require a sign and the Greeks seek after wisdom: But we preach Christ crucified, unto the Jews a stumblingblock, and unto the Greeks foolishness" (1:19-23).

> "Because the foolishness of God is wiser than men; and the weakness of God is stronger than men. For ye see your calling, brethren, how that not many wise men after the flesh, not many mighty, not many noble, are called: But God hath chosen the foolish things of the world to confound the wise; and God hath chosen the weak things of the world to confound the things which are mighty" (1:25-27).

47

This contrast between the wisdom of God and of man is further pointed out in I Corinthians 3:18-20:

> "Let no man deceive himself. If any man among you seemeth to be wise in this world, let him become a fool, that he may be wise. For the wisdom of this world is foolishness with God. For it is written, He taketh the wise in their own craftiness. And again, The Lord knoweth the thoughts of the wise, that they are vain."

The prophecy of Obadiah 8 does not suggest that God is going to destroy the wise men. The implication rather is that He will bring their wisdom and understanding to naught. Job 5:12-13 throws light on this principle:

> "He disappointeth the devices of the crafty, so that their hands cannot perform their enterprise. He taketh the wise in their own craftiness: and the counsel of the froward is carried headlong."

There are numerous illustrations in Scripture of the all-wise God bringing the counsel of wise men to a shameful end. Perhaps the story of Ahithophel recorded in II Samuel 15-17 best illustrates the point. These chapters record the days of Absalom's uprising against his father David. Ahithophel's counsel was highly regarded by both David and Absalom. In fact, his advice was received as "the oracle of God."

He counselled Absalom as to how David could be captured. His counsel was good but God brought it to naught through the advice of Hushai. Hushai advised a different plan of attack which Absalom accepted. The plan failed and we are told that it failed because the "Lord had appointed to defeat the good counsel of Ahithophel, to the intent that the Lord might bring evil upon Absalom." When, therefore, Ahithophel saw that his counsel was not followed, he went to his home, put his house in order, and hung himself.

Isaiah says of God, "It is he that sitteth upon the circle of the earth, and the inhabitants thereof are as grasshoppers; that stretcheth out the heavens as a curtain, and spreadeth them out as a tent to dwell in; That bringeth the princes to nothing; he maketh the judges of the earth as vanity" (40:22, 23). He also says that God is He who "frustrateth the tokens of the liars, and maketh diviners mad; that turneth wise men backward, and maketh their knowledge foolish" (44:25).

The Psalmist says, "The Lord bringeth the counsel of the heathen to naught: he maketh the devices of the people of none effect" (33:10).

The Gospels and the book of Acts also give illustrations of "wise men" endeavoring to destroy the program of God, only to find their shrewdest plots destroyed.

The prophet Jeremiah has an important word for all wise men of all ages:

> "Thus saith the Lord, Let not the wise man glory in his wisdom, neither let the mighty man glory in his might, let not the rich man glory in his riches: But let him that glorieth glory in this, that he understandeth and knoweth me, that I am the Lord which exercise loving-kindness, judgment, and righteousness, in the earth: for in these things I delight, saith the Lord" (9:23, 24).

> *"And thy mighty men, O Teman, shall be dismayed, to the end that every one of the mount of Esau may be cut off by slaughter"* (*Obadiah 9*).

Jeremiah adds a descriptive picture to this prophecy concerning the overthrow of Edom's mighty men. He says, ". . . and at that day shall the heart of the mighty men of Edom be as the heart of a woman in her pangs" (49:22).

The modern term "military leaders" best describes the "mighty men" of Bible times.

They were heroes who had accomplished some spectacular victories. It will be recalled that David gathered mighty men around him. There was Jashobeam, a chief of the captains who had "lifted up his spear against three hundred slain by him at one time" (I Chronicles 11:11). There was Benaiah "who had done many acts; he slew two lionlike men of Moab: also he went down and slew a lion in a pit in a snowy day" (I Chronicles 11:22). "And he slew an Egyptian, a man of great stature, five cubits high; and in the Egyptian's hand was a spear like a weaver's beam; and he went down to him with a staff, and plucked the spear out of the Egyptian's hand, and slew him with his own spear" (I Chronicles 11:23).

But the victory of the Lord does not always fall to those of greatest physical strength or military might. In the economy of God, it is not what you have but whose you are that determines victory. The Old Testament teaches us that a right relationship with the Almighty is basic to victory. There were times when Israel had numerical superiority but lost her battles. There were other times when she was far outnumbered by her enemies but was victorious. Her relationship with God made the difference.

Cursed is the man who trusts in the arm of flesh. Blessed is he who learns that he can be more than conqueror through Jesus Christ. It is but a little thing with God to overcome with few or with many.

In those hours of insecurity and impending defeat, one ought to read II Chronicles 20 and follow the example of Jehoshaphat. On the other hand, when feelings of self-sufficiency take over the same chapter should be read from the view of the experience of the children of Moab, Ammon, and mount Seir.

# Chapter VI

## THE MESSAGE OF OBADIAH

### The Cause of Judgment

*"For thy violence against thy brother Jacob shame shall cover thee, and thou shalt be cut off forever" (Obadiah 10).*

Retribution is the subject of this verse. It introduces us to the specific reason for God's judgment against the Edomites. The cause of it was their cruel and persistent violence against God's people. We will note a partial description of their cruelty in verses 11-14.

It must be remembered that it is a "righteous thing with God to recompense tribulation to" those who trouble his people (II Thessalonians 1:6). God "keepeth covenant and mercy with them that love Him and keep His commandments," but He repays those who "hate Him to their face, to destroy them . . ." (Deuteronomy 7:9, 10).

The Psalmist says of the wicked, "His mischief shall return upon his own head, and his violent dealing shall come down upon his own pate" (7:16). God is a consuming fire. He will in no wise allow the unrepentant to go unpunished. He has established a law whereby sin brings its own judgment for "whatsoever a man sows, that shall he also reap." Sin has a way of finding men out. There remains for the unrighteous "a certain fearful looking for of judgment and fiery indignation, which shall devour the adversaries" (Hebrews 10:27). It is indeed a "fearful thing to fall into the hands of the living God" (Hebrews 10:31). Retribution and recompense belong unto God.

The ultimate fulfillment of this prophecy, "thou shalt be cut off forever," did not take place until A.D. 70. Though Edom was destroyed as a national power long before that, the Edomites did not disappear from the scene of history until the Roman destruction of Jerusalem.

The complete annihilation of the Edomite nation points up a significant distinction between God's judgments on His people and His judgments on the godless. He judges His own people to discipline and correct them, thus bringing them unto Himself. His judgments on the ungodly are to separate them from Him. He punishes His own to purify them. He cuts off those who are godless and defiled for the same purpose a doctor amputates an infected and diseased limb.

Obadiah "intimates that the calamity would not be only for a time as in the case of Israel, but that the Lord would execute such a punishment as would prove that the Idumeans were aliens to Him; for God in chastening His church ever observes certain limits, and He never forgets His covenant" (Calvin).

> *"In the day that thou stoodest on the other side, in the day that strangers carried away captive his forces, and foreigners entered into his gates and cast lots upon Jerusalem, even thou wast as one of them" (Obadiah 11).*

Jesus tells us of a priest and a Levite who passed by on the other side. They deliberately avoided involvement in helping a man in need. It was within their power to save a brother from death but they refused. It was finally left to a man of another race (Samaritan) to show the way of love and mercy.

The attitude of the Edomites toward their brethren the Israelites was even worse than that of the priest and Levite. They were not content to pass by on the other side. They joined Israel's enemies and assisted them in their vicious plundering and murdering.

Like the Roman soldiers who cast lots for the garment of Him who hung on Calvary's cross, the Edomites cast in their lot for a share in the spoils of Jerusalem.

It is as if the Moslems should rise up against the Christians and fellow Christians should join the Moslems in a ruthless slaughter of the Christians. It is the picture of venting one's animosity against a brother who is already badly beaten. It is the story of kicking a fallen and helpless relative who is bleeding to death.

It could be said of the people of Edom as was said by our Lord in His day of Israel, "I was hungered and you fed me not, naked and you clothed me not, sick and you visited me not. . . ." Edom not only neglected the things she should do, she also did the things she should not do.

"Edom is the type of all enemies of the Lord, whose hatred against Him is manifested in various ways, from standing aloof, in more or less polite refusal to have anything to do with God's church, to mockery, persecution, and blasphemous desecration of God's holy institutions" (Laetsch).

As children of God, we constantly have to guard against being "as one of them." Through our unwillingness to speak up or to become involved in the never-ending struggle against the evil forces which surround us, we can easily become "as one of them." In attitude or action, passively or actively, it is an easy thing to follow the path of least resistance — to become "as one of them."

> *"But thou shouldest not have looked on the day of thy brother in the day that he became a stranger; neither shouldest thou have rejoiced over the children of Judah in the day of their destruction; neither shouldest thou have spoken proudly in the day of distress. Thou shouldest not have entered into the gate of my people in the day of their calamity; yea, thou shouldest not have looked on their affliction in the day of their calamity, nor have laid hands on their substance in the day of their calamity; Neither shouldest thou have stood in the crossway, to cut off those of his that did escape; neither shouldest thou have delivered up those of his that did remain in the day of distress" (Obadiah 12-14).*

Israel's terrible suffering is framed in these phrases:

    . . . the day he became a stranger
    . . . the day of their destruction
    . . . the day of distress (twice)
    . . . the day of their calamity (thrice).

Deep, dark, and devastating tragedy has struck the household of Israel with destroying force. This is no time for any expression of casual indifference on the part of friends or relatives. Much less is it a time to add to Israel's misery. But this is the very thing the Edomites did. They gazed upon

53

and gloated over the sufferings of Jacob's descendants. They looked with disdain and scorn on their own bruised and dying relatives, the Israelites.

"Malicious gazing," says Pusey, "on human calamity, forgetful of man's common origin and common liability to ill is the worst form of human hate. It was one of the contumelies of the Cross."

Ellicott says the behavior of the Edomites reminds us again "of the wanton and savage insolence around the Cross."

The prophet uses the following verbs to describe the sin of the Edomites: looking on, rejoicing over, speaking proudly (vs. 12), entering in, laying hands on (v. 13), standing in, and delivering up (v. 14). They were a people with calloused hearts, cruel hands, and depraved minds.

This is uninhibited hate in action. It is no doubt also a picture of that which would happen to the Israelites today if the Arab nations could have their way.

The Psalmist accuses the Edomites of seeking the utter destruction of Jerusalem: "Raze it, raze it, even to the foundation thereof," was their battlecry (137:7). Amos insists that the punishment of God will fall on Edom "because he did pursue his brother with a sword, and did cast off all pity and his anger did tear perpetually, and he kept his wrath forever" (1:11).

The Edomites not only watched the destruction of Jerusalem and the massacre of its inhabitants, they joined hands with the destroyer. They stole and looted from the helpless and then stood in the crossroads to deliver into the hand of the enemy any who might escape.

This behavior of the Edomites stands in bold contrast to the directives given several centuries later by the Son of God to the descendants of Jacob, when He said, "You have heard that it hath been said, Thou shalt love thy neighbor, and hate thine enemy. But I say unto you, Love your enemies, bless them that curse you, do good to them that hate you, and pray for them which despitefully use you, and persecute you; that ye may be the children of your Father which is in heaven: for He maketh His sun to rise on the evil and on the good and sendeth rain on the just and on the unjust" (Matthew 6:43-45).

To love one's neighbor as one's self is the fruit and the proof of loving God with all one's heart. Conversely, to hate one's brother is murder. And this spirit of murder remained in the lineage of the Edomites until the last member was slain.

The Herods of Jesus' day were Edomites (Idumeans). It was because of their hatred of the Jews that Rome put them in places of authority. Their murderous hatred is a black picture. Herod the Great slaughtered the Jewish babies at the time of Jesus' birth. Herod Antipas killed John the Baptist, while Herod Agrippa killed James and imprisoned Peter with the intent of killing him.

The whole history of Edomite behavior beginning with Esau and concluding with Herod stands in bold contrast to those great principles of love so adequately defined in the New Testament.

"Charity suffereth long, and is kind; charity envieth not; charity vaunteth not itself, is not puffed up, Doth not behave itself unseemly, seeketh not her own, is not easily provoked, thinketh no evil; Rejoiceth not in iniquity, but rejoiceth in the truth; Beareth all things, believeth all things, hopeth all things, endureth all things" (I Corinthians 13:4-7).

*"For the day of the Lord is near upon all the heathen: as thou hast done, it shall be done unto thee: thy reward shall return upon thine own head. For as ye have drunk upon my holy mountain, so shall all the heathen drink continually, yea, they shall drink, and they shall swallow down, and they shall be as though they had not been"* (*Obadiah 15, 16*).

The subject of the day of the Lord is vast and can only be touched on in this commentary. Suffice it to say that the many Scriptures which deal with the subject overwhelmingly point to judgment on the nations.

Joel gives us an excellent description of the day of the Lord. He first describes it as a day of destruction.

"Alas, for the day! for the day of the Lord is at hand, and as a destruction from the Almighty shall it come" (1:15).

Then in Chapter 2, verse 2, Joel adds:

"A day of darkness and gloominess, a day of clouds and of thick darkness. . . ."

Again in Joel 3:13, 14, we read:

"Put ye in the sickle, for the harvest is ripe: come, get you down; for the press is full, the fats overflow; for their wickedness is great. Multitudes, multitudes in the valley of decision: for the day of the Lord is near in the valley of decision."

These passages teach us that the day of the Lord is a day of destruction, darkness, and decision. The idea of decision is not that of a multitude being given the privilege of making up their minds as to which way to turn. It is the picture of a judge's decision. It is the day of verdict. It may be likened unto the day in which the death angel passed over Egypt. The decision was made, the verdict handed down, and the judgment was to fall.

The New Testament describes the day of the Lord as that time in which God will take vengeance on those who know Him not and who obey not His Gospel (II Thessalonians 1:8). It is a day that will come as a thief in the night, "in the which the heavens shall pass away with a great noise, and the elements shall melt with fervent heat, the earth also and the works that are therein shall be burned up" (II Peter 3:10).

"For yourselves know perfectly that the day of the Lord so cometh as a thief in the night. For when they shall say, Peace and safety; then sudden destruction cometh upon them, as travail upon a woman with child; and they shall not escape. But ye, brethren, are not in darkness, that that day should overtake you as a thief" (I Thessalonians 5:2-4).

John vividly pictures it in Revelation 6:16, 17, as the great day of God's wrath. A day in which men will hide themselves in the dens and among the rocks and then call upon the mountains to fall on them and hide them from the wrath of the Lamb.

It is well to remember that the wrath of God (and, hence, the day of the Lord) is both contemporary and future — it is both current and coming. The wrath of God has always been upon the ungodly. The Bible speaks of men storing up unto themselves "wrath against the day of wrath and revelation of the righteous judgment of God" (Rom. 2:5). John 3:36, Romans 1:18, and Ephesians 2:3 throw added light on this fact.

For the Edomites the day of the Lord came to them in a period of history which culminated in A.D. 70. For other heathen peoples, nations, and empires, *their* day of the Lord has come at other times in history. It is, therefore, correct to refer to the day of the Lord as being current. It is, however, just as accurate to point to a future time in which God will bring final judgment upon all the ungodly and unrighteous.

As the Edomites had done unto the Israelites so it would be returned upon their own heads. As they had defiled God's holy mountain in drinking of the wine of their own implacable hate against Israel thereon, so they and all other heathen nations would drink of the wine of God's wrath.

The prophet Jeremiah says,

> "For thus saith the Lord God of Israel unto me; take the wine cup of His fury at my hand, and cause all the nations, to whom I send thee, to drink it. And they shall drink, and be moved, and be mad, because of the sword that I will send among them. . . . Drink ye and be drunken, and spue, and fall, and rise no more, because of the sword which I will send among you" (25:15, 16, 27).

Edom is one of the nations (v. 21) commanded to drink of the wrath of God in its prophecy of Jeremiah.

Chapter VII

# THE MESSAGE OF OBADIAH

*The Consummation of Judgment*

*"But upon mount Zion shall be deliverance, and there shall be holiness; and the house of Jacob shall possess their possessions" ('Obadiah 17).*

The prophetic scene here takes a drastic change. The destruction of the Edomites no longer holds the place of prominence. The restoration of Israel and the exaltation of the kingdom of the Lord are brought to the center of the stage. It points to Jerusalem's coronation day. Jacob's descendants are brought into their own, no longer to be trodden under the feet of other nations.

"Thank God," says Petrie, "for the double picture; doomed Edom and restored Israel. The fulfillment of the first bids us wait for the sure fulfillment of the second. The pictures are carved by the same hand. They are inspired by the same Spirit." As Edom was destroyed, so Israel will be restored. And there seems to be every evidence of the fulfilling of this prophecy of restoration today. Coming events are casting their shadows.

"This part of Obadiah's vision is an exquisite cameo of Jewish hope. In these five verses (17-21) are included all the basic features of Israel's waiting glory. We are not surprised then to learn that Obadiah is one of the favorite books of the Jews. As the Christian gathers strength from the Master's promises and leans on them . . . so the Jew cheers his thumping heart by the last five verses of Obadiah. In his eye this is the golden page of Hebrew prophecy. It is bright with heaven and Israel's hope" (Petrie).

Israel's Mount Zion (vv. 17, 21) stands in bold contrast to Edom's mount of Esau (vv. 8, 9, 19, 21). As we have already learned, the mount of Esau refers to a rugged mountainous area south of the Dead Sea. Its major cities of

Bozrah and Petra were almost impregnable. This area was known for its commerce, conflicts, and conquests. It is a symbol of the secular and the sensual; of the world in all of its independence of God.

Mount Zion, on the other hand, is a hill on which part of Jerusalem is built. It is often used synonymously in the Scriptures with Jerusalem. It is vulnerable to attack and has no natural protection. In spite of this, it is God's holy hill. It stands for all that is holy and righteous. It is the Old Testament center of the worship of Jehovah. Isaiah says, "For Zion's sake will I not hold my peace, and for Jerusalem's sake I will not rest, until the righteousness thereof go forth as brightness, and the salvation thereof as a lamp that burneth" (62:1).

As David once reigned on Mount Zion, so his great Son shall some day reign. He will come with a strong hand and His arm will rule for Him. He the Holy One of Israel will restore the glory of Jerusalem and rule the nations with a rod of iron. "Therefore the redeemed of the Lord shall return, and come with singing unto Zion; and everlasting joy shall be upon their head; they shall obtain gladness and joy; and sorrow and mourning shall flee away" (Isaiah 51:11).

The key words of Obadiah 17 are *deliverance, holiness,* and *possessions.* These three words outline the whole history of Israel.

A. *Possessions*

It was the purpose of God to set Israel "on high above all nations of the earth" (Deuteronomy 28:1). They were God's chosen earthly people. They were to dwell in a land that would flow with milk and honey. They were to be a people of great possessions. Note God's promise of blessings upon them.

> "Blessed shalt thou be in the city, and blessed shalt thou be in the field. Blessed shall be the fruit of thy body, and the fruit of thy ground, and the fruit of thy cattle, the increase of thy kine, and the flocks of thy sheep. Blessed shall be thy basket and thy store. Blessed shalt thou be when thou comest in, and blessed shalt thou be when thou goest out. The Lord shall cause thine enemies that rise up against thee to be smitten before thy face: they shall come out against thee one way, and

flee before thee seven ways. The Lord shall command the blessing upon thee in thy storehouses, and in all that thou settest thine hand unto; and he shall bless thee in the land which the Lord thy God giveth thee. The Lord shall establish thee an holy people unto himself, as he hath sworn unto thee, if thou shalt keep the commandments of the Lord thy God, and walk in his ways. And all people of the earth shall see that thou art called by the name of the Lord; and they shall be afraid of thee. And the Lord shall make thee plenteous in goods, in the fruit of thy body, and in the fruit of thy cattle, and in the fruit of thy ground, in the land which the Lord sware unto thy fathers to give thee. The Lord shall open unto thee his good treasure, the heaven to give the rain unto thy land in his season, and to bless all the work of thine hand: and thou shalt lend unto many nations, and thou shalt not borrow. And the Lord shall make thee the head, and not the tail; and thou shalt not be beneath; if that thou hearken unto the commandments of the Lord thy God, which I command thee this day, to observe and to do them: And thou shalt not go aside from any of the words which I command thee this day, to the right hand, or to the left, to go after other gods to serve them" (Deuteronomy 28:3-14).

The purpose of God's blessing upon His chosen people is expressly stated in these words, "And all the people of the earth shall see that thou art called by the name of the Lord."

### B. *Holiness*

It must be remembered that Israel's possessions were conditional. They were to enjoy the blessings of God on the basis of their obedience to His commands. Their obedience in turn was to reveal the holiness of Him who said, "Sanctify yourselves therefore and be ye holy; for I am the Lord your God" (Leviticus 20:7). Holiness was to characterize the people of Israel.

### C. *Deliverance*

Unfortunately, Israel repeatedly disobeyed the voice of the Lord and was, therefore, repeatedly disciplined. The Israelites often yielded to the idolatry of pagan neighbors and, hence, the curse of God was brought upon them. The book of Judges records numerous instances in which God allowed His chosen people to be overrun by pagan nations because of their waywardness. In turn the Lord again and again delivered them when they turned to Him in repentance.

But the day came when Israel's backslidings seemed beyond repair. Then according to His word, God allowed Israel to be "removed into all the kingdoms of the earth." However, He had long before made a covenant with David concerning Zion, David's throne. And Obadiah has added his word concerning the fact that the kingdom would be restored and mount Zion would once more become a place of blessing.

In Obadiah's day such a prophecy looked like the wildest of dreams. Edom was in the place of supremacy and Israel was a defeated and devastated nation. But just as surely as the Edomites were destroyed so deliverance, holiness, and possessions will be restored to the house of Jacob.

> *"And the house of Jacob shall be a fire, and the house of Joseph a flame and the house of Esau for stubble and they shall kindle in them, and devour them; and there shall not be any remaining at the house of Esau; for the Lord hath spoken it" (Obadiah 18).*

Amos adds the weight of his witness concerning the conflagration which was to devour Edom.

> "Thus saith the Lord; For three transgressions of Edom, and for four, I will not turn away the punishment thereof; because he did pursue his brother with the sword, and did cast off all pity, and his anger did tear perpetually, and he kept his wrath for ever: But I will send a fire upon Teman, which shall devour the palaces of Bozrah" (1:11, 12).

In God's plan of judgment all things ultimately have to face the test of fire. But how hollow it must have sounded in Obadiah's day to have anyone talk about the house of Esau burning like stubble. And how unlikely it appeared that the flame would come from the house of Jacob. Israel itself was little more than a dying ember at the time this prophecy was made. But God has ways of fulfilling His purposes even when it takes the casting down of some and the raising up of others. What "the Lord has spoken" is as well as accomplished. In the counsel of the eternal God, the house of Jacob was already a fire and the house of Esau burned and devoured stubble.

It is well for every child of God to remember that "every man's work shall be manifest: for the day shall declare it, because it shall be revealed by fire; and the fire shall try every man's work of what sort it is" (I Corinthians 3:13). How important it then is to build with gold, silver, and precious stone that we may not suffer loss in the judgment.

It is noteworthy that there has been no trace of the household of Esau for almost two thousand years. Like the Philistines, the Moabites, the Ammonites, and other pagan enemies of Israel, the descendants of Jacob's twin brother have long since been extinct. ". . . and there shall not be any remaining of the house of Esau" is a prophecy perfectly fulfilled.

On the other hand, it is a recorded historical fact that empires and nations have made repeated efforts to destroy the descendants of Jacob only to have them remain unassimilated and undestroyed. The Jewish people stand as a miracle of the centuries and as an irrefutable evidence of fulfilled prophecy.

> *"And they of the south shall possess the mount of Esau; and they of the plain the Philistines; and they shall possess the fields of Ephraim, and the fields of Samaria: and Benjamin shall possess Gilead. And the captivity of this host of the children of Israel shall possess that of the Canaanites, even unto Zarephath; and the captivity of Jerusalem, which is in Sepharad, shall possess the cities of the south"* (*Obadiah 19, 20*).

The word "captivity" (used twice in verse 20) is more accurately translated "exiles." This clarification is important to the understanding of the verse.

The Old Testament prophets are unanimous in their declaration of the return of Israel to Palestine. They join Obadiah in his prophecy that all the territory given by God to Abraham, Isaac, and Jacob will some day be repossessed. And like Obadiah, they made their prophetic statements in days in which any hope of fulfillment looked utterly impossible.

Eight hundred and fifty years before Christ, Amos wrote,

"And I will bring again the captivity of my people of Israel, and they shall build the waste cities, and inhabit them; and they shall plant vineyards, and drink the wine thereof; they shall also make gardens, and eat the fruit of them. And I will plant them upon their land, and they shall no more be pulled up out of their land which I have given them, saith the Lord thy God" (Amos 9:14, 15).

Centuries before Amos, Moses' inspired pen had written,

"Then the Lord thy God will turn thy captivity, and have compassion upon thee, and will return and gather thee from all the nations, whither the Lord hath scattered thee" (Deuteronomy 30:30).

Isaiah and Jeremiah, Zephaniah and Zechariah also had something to say about this:

"And it shall come to pass in that day, that the Lord shall set his hand again the second time to recover the remnant of his people which shall be left, from Assyria, and from Egypt, and from Pathros, and from Cush, and from Elam, and from Shinar, and from Hamath, and from the islands of the sea" (Isaiah 11:11).

"But, the Lord liveth, that brought up the children of Israel from the land of the north, and from all the lands whither he had driven them: and I will bring them again into their land that I gave unto their fathers" (Jeremiah 16:15).

"And I will gather the remnant of my flock out of all countries whither I have driven them, and will bring them again to their folds; and they shall be fruitful and increase" (Jeremiah 23:3).

"At that time will I bring you again, even in the time that I gather you: for I will make you a name and a praise among all people of the earth, when I turn back your captivity before your eyes, saith the Lord" (Zephaniah 3:20).

63

"I will bring them again also out of the land of Egypt, and gather them out of Assyria; and I will bring them into the land of Gilead and Lebanon; and place shall not be found for them" (Zechariah 10:10).

Laetsch believes the promises of verses 19 and 20 of Obadiah have a spiritual fulfillment. He says, "Matthew and Mark tell us that people from Jerusalem, Judea, Galilee, and beyond Jordan, Decapolis, Idumea, Tyre, and Sidon were gained for Christ's kingdom by Christ's preaching. The book of Acts records the conquest of the countries and districts named in Obadiah by the church, the true mount Zion; Philistia (Obadiah 19) in Acts 8:40; 9:32-43; Samaria in Acts 8:5-17; Zarephath in Phoenicia, Acts 11:19; Sepharad in Asia Minor, Revelation 3:1, and Paul's activity. Paul was a Benjamite, and Benjamin is named as possessing Gilead and at Paul's time Gilead was a mixed population of Jews and Gentiles, representative of conditions under which Paul labored in the world at large."

> *"And saviours shall come up on mount Zion to judge the mount of Esau; and the kingdom shall be the Lord's" (Obadiah 21).*

The word "saviours" is generally understood by Jewish scholars to mean deliverers or judges. Judges 3:9 suggests the picture:

> "And when the children of Israel cried unto the Lord, the Lord raised up a deliverer to the children of Israel, who delivered them, even Othniel the son of Kenaz, Caleb's younger brother."

Nehemiah says,

> "Therefore thou deliveredst them into the hand of their enemies, who vexed them: and in the time of their trouble, when they cried unto thee, thou heardest them from heaven, and according to thy manifold mercies thou gavest them saviours, who saved them out of the hand of their enemies" (9:27).

"And it shall come to pass," says Joel, "that whosoever shall call on the name of the Lord shall be delivered:

for in mount Zion and in Jerusalem shall be deliverance, as the Lord hath said, and in the remnant whom the Lord shall call" (2:32).

*"And the kingdom shall be the Lord's,"* is another way of saying, "and the Lord shall be king." Not a few of the prophets expressed their faith in a coming theocracy in which God would rule as Lord of lords, and King of kings. It was left, however, to the Son of God himself and the book of the Revelation to reveal the full glory of that kingdom.

Daniel predicted a day in which the God of heaven would set up a kingdom, "which shall never be destroyed" (2:44).

Zechariah says, "And the Lord shall be king over all the earth: in that day shall there be one Lord, and His name one" (14:9).

The angel's message to the virgin Mary was, "And He shall reign over the house of Jacob forever and of his kingdom there shall be no end" (Luke 1:33).

John the Revelator tells of hearing great voices in heaven saying, "The kingdoms of this world are become the kingdom of our Lord and of His Christ; and He shall reign for ever and ever" (Revelation 3:11).

It is probable that the Old Testament prophets did not see the full extent of that glorious kingdom in which God would take unto Himself His own great power and reign over men. But they saw enough to make them long for the day when the kingdom and the kingship would be the Lord's.

"Jehovah is and remains supreme in His kingdom of power," says Laetsch, "governing the affairs of the world; and in His kingdom of grace, ruling, blessing, and extending His church, and all its individual members and leading them finally into His kingdom of glory (Rev. 21 and 22). In spite of all oppositions of the forces of hell (Ps. 2:1-3), Jehovah is and remains King of kings and Lord of lords! In time and in eternity, Jehovah's is the kingdom!"

In that day when His kingdom is revealed, the four and twenty elders will fall on their faces and worship God saying, "We give thee thanks, O Lord God Almighty, which art and wast and art to come; because thou hast taken to thee thy great power, and hast reigned" (Revelation 11:17).

May God hasten that day.

# Chapter VIII

## OBADIAH SPEAKS TODAY

Does Obadiah have a message for men of the twentieth century? Is it possible that something written centuries ago can be meaningful today? Certainly with all the academic, scientific, and sociological changes that have taken place through the centuries, one has the right to ask such questions.

One answer is found in the fact that though decades, centuries, and millenniums have ways of changing most things, there are some things that remain invariable. There are the immutable principles of truth which abide forever. And there is a sense of the word in which all significant advance is built upon the unchangeable.

Two of the invariables of time are the character of God and the character of man. We need not argue the case relative to the immutability of God's character. But perhaps we need to remind ourselves that the essential characteristics of fallen human nature have not changed from Adam's time to today. Though circumstances, situations, and sociological conditions have changed, though advances have been made in the physical, academic, economic and scientific fields, human nature is still that same paradoxical mixture of love and hate, goodness and evil, God-thirsting and God-hating.

Because the book of Obadiah is a message from God to man, it is reasonable to expect that that which God has said to man in it can apply to man today. We look, therefore, to the Old Testament writers, not simply to give us historical accounts of what has happened in God's dealings with men in the past but for lessons we can learn today. And the Bible has already informed us that these things are written for our profit and learning. Let us consider then several lessons from the book of Obadiah.

1. *God is not unmindful of the behavior of the godless.*

Neither godless men nor nations are accomplishing things

behind His back. He neither slumbers nor sleeps. His omniscient eye misses nothing.

The history of nations certainly confirms the Old Testament prophets in this regard. They prophesied the rise and fall of both nations and empires. Their prophecies were fulfilled. God is the God of nations and He raises up one and sets down another.

## 2. *God will bring ultimate judgment on the godless.*

In all conflicts, He will have the last word. There is a horrible finality to God's judgment upon nations. It has been left to the archaeologist's spade to dig artifacts from the crumbling dust of nations upon whom God through His prophets pronounced judgment. Search as you may today for the descendants of Edom, your search will be in vain. And needless to say, Edom is only one illustration of many given in the Holy Scriptures.

## 3. *God's compassion is never fully removed from His own people.*

Though this is not the subject with which Obadiah basically deals, yet the promises of Israel's restoration recorded therein clearly suggests this fact. Whom God loves, He chastises. But chastisement is always for correction, never for destruction.

It is noteworthy that God often allows the godless to chastise the godly. This theme is clearly revealed in the prophet Amos. And how evident this fact is in Obadiah's account of Edom's behavior toward Israel. But in the end God destroys the scourge with which He punishes His people.

The Psalmist brings this thought into sharp focus. Concerning the descendants of David to whom God had given a covenant of blessing, it is written,

> "If his children forsake my law, and walk not in my judgments; if they break my statutes, and keep not my commandments; then will I visit their transgression with the rod, and their iniquity with stripes. Nevertheless, my lovingkindness will I not utterly take from him, nor suffer my faithfulness to fail. My covenant will I not break, nor alter the thing that is gone out of my lips" (89:30-34).

### 4. Pride is the basis of man's misbehavior both toward God and man.

"The pride of thine heart hath deceived thee," says Obadiah. We have already said much about pride in an earlier chapter and, hence, will not add more here. It is sufficient to remember that Obadiah gives us an easily-understood object lesson on the subject of pride and its dangers.

### 5. Earthly security will fail in the hour of God's judgment.

All man-made fortresses are built on sand. They are destined to crumble and decay. Cursed is the man who trusts in the arm of flesh. The Edomites had all that was necessary to bolster self-confidence. Their military situation seemed impregnable. But they had taken God's goodness for granted. They had not reckoned upon His hatred of iniquity and unrighteousness. They had closed their eyes to all that history could teach them and their ears to the prophets of God.

And in these days when men and nations bow the knee to military might, the message of Obadiah needs to be reconsidered. In these days in which we have built security upon the dollar, we need to rethink the fact that man shall not live by bread alone.

### 6. Hatred leads to heinous behavior.

We have observed the cruelty of the Edomites in their relationship with the Israelites. We are tempted to ask, "How can the human heart become so callous?" But no man will ever live so long that he does not need to be reminded that murder itself springs from the root of hate. Like all other roots, it will grow and bring forth fruit if it is not torn out. How drastically the child of God should deal with any root of bitterness, envy, jealousy, or hatred he may find in the soil of his heart. If he does not destroy it, it will destroy him.

### 7. We must beware of the sins of omission.

The cruel, overt acts of the Edomites began by a refusal to become involved in helping those in need. At first, they stood back and watched. In this, they became guilty by association. Nor did it take long until their own hands were taking an active part in the horrible slaughter of the Israelites. A refusal to stand for that which is right gives assent to that which is evil.

8. *God communicates with His children and forewarns them through His prophets.*

Through this it becomes plain that He knows the end from the beginning.

The omniscience of God is taught in the Scriptures both explicitly and implicitly. God is the Alpha and Omega of time and the Eternal One. He is the eternal contemporary with whom there is no past, present, or future. This is why He could have mercy on sinful men centuries before the cross and why that same mercy is effective centuries after the cross. The cross is a timeless fact with God. The Lamb was slain in His eyes before the foundation of the world. The sacrifice of Christ spans all of eternity.

It is this Omniscient One who communicates with men and informs them of things to come. And fulfilled prophecy is one of the irrefutable arguments for the inspiration of the Scriptures. David H. Johnson presents this fact in the following interesting fashion.

"You are familiar with the fact that if you make one forecast, the likelihood of being correct is one out of two possibilities. Suppose you predict that it will rain in your city tomorrow morning, you have one chance out of two of being correct. It either will rain or it will not rain in the morning. Suppose you add one more prediction and say that in addition to rain in the forenoon, there will be clear, sunny weather prevailing in the afternoon. You now have one chance out of four of being correct. Your morning prediction may be correct, and the afternoon prediction incorrect; or your morning prediction may be wrong and your afternoon prediction may be right; or you may have missed both of these predictions. To attain your goal, both of your predictions must be fulfilled.

"Should you add a third prediction for the evening and forecast that there will be a tremendous change in the weather, with the temperature dropping 40° during the night from the highest temperature of the previous day, you now have one chance out of eight, for there are eight possibilities, with only one of that number resulting in the fulfillment of all your forecasts.

"If you added still another, making four predictions, you would then have one chance out of sixteen of winning your goal. If you made five predictions, your chances of being correct in all five would be one out of thirty-two. In other words, every time you add an element of prediction, you reduce your chances of being right by one-half. Each time you add one new prediction you double the number of possibilities.

"Applying this mathematical rule to the Bible, with its scores and scores of prophetic statements, you will readily understand that if the Bible were not God's inspired Word, it would soon show up.

"By considering fifty prophecies or predictions, what chance does anyone have of seeing that number fulfilled at a subsequent time or times? When you set forth forty prophecies, there is only one chance out of 1,099,511,627,776 possibilities of being right. When you increase the number to fifty, you then have one chance out of 1,125,899,906,842,624 possibilities that all fifty predictions will be fulfilled. And, of course, there are many more than fifty prophetic statements in God's Word.

"If the Bible were not the inspired Word of God and if the prophetic utterances lacked divine origin, surely the Bible long ago would have demonstrated itself to be ridiculous. If it were a book of human intelligence with God left out, it would today be a discarded volume of folklore and myths. On the other hand, by the fulfillment of prophecies the Bible demonstrates that it must be and is the inspired Word of God."

9. *God is Lord and reigns over all.*

The Israelites of Obadiah's day had many apparent reasons to question the sovereignty of God. They failed to take into consideration the basic reasons for their sufferings. They refused to relate their chastisements to their sins and, hence, did not turn to God in repentance. They limited the Holy One of Israel by their behavior. For this reason, God no longer appeared to be the Lord of Hosts.

But the Bible claims and history demonstrates the fact that God reigns in the kingdom of men even when the godless claim He is dead and when the godly feel He is silent and unconcerned.

One's appreciation of the sovereignty of God in the world is colored by the degree to which He is Lord in the individual life. We see more clearly the ruling hand of God on earth when we experience His ruling hand in our lives.

It is the writer to the Philippians who tells us that God has exalted Christ and given Him a name above all names and that at the name of Christ every knee shall bow and every tongue confess that Jesus Christ is Lord to the glory of God. He who gives to the Saviour a place and name in his own life above all other names does not find it difficult to believe that God is on His throne and will establish His kingdom for ever and ever.

10. *We need to beware of the Esaus in our own lives.*

Obadiah has given to us a two-fold message:

    a. Historically — a message against Edom with its side application to all godless nations.

    b. Allegorically — a message against the spirit of Esau within every man. Edom is a type of the Adamic nature and of all that is carnal and profane.

Harry Ironsides has said, "The Edomites represent the fleshly and all that is carnal. And the carnal mind is ever the enemy of the new life imparted to the children of God, because it is not subject to the law of God. In its very nature it cannot be for it rejoices in impiety and lifts up its haughty head in defiance of all that is holy. How much sorrow and secret anguish has its presence cost every conscientious saint. But soon it shall be cast down to rise no more; soon the bodies of our humiliation will be made like unto the body of Christ's glory. . . ."

The struggle which took place in Rebecca's womb between Esau and Jacob is symbolic not only of the centuries' long conflict between the Edomites and the Israelites but also of the continuing battle in the heart of every Christian between his old and new natures. Furthermore, as Esau the firstborn was the carnal one so in our lives, "that was not first which is spiritual, but that which is natural; and afterward that which is spiritual" (I Corinthians 15:46).

We see this truth in clear perspective in Galatians 5:17-25, and Romans 6:6-14:

71

"For we naturally love to do evil things that are just the opposite from the things that the Holy Spirit tells us to do; and the good things we want to do when the Spirit has His way with us are just the opposite of our natural desires. These two forces within us are constantly fighting each other to win control over us and our wishes are never free from their pressures. When you are guided by the Holy Spirit you need no longer force yourself to obey Jewish laws. But when you follow your own wrong inclinations your lives will produce these evil results: impure thoughts; eagerness for lustful pleasure; Idolatry, spiritism (that is, encouraging the activity of demons); hatred and fighting; jealousy and anger; constant effort to get the best for yourself; complaints and criticisms; the feeling that everyone else is wrong except those in your own little group; and there will be wrong doctrine, Envy, murder, drunkenness, wild parties and all that sort of thing. Let me tell you again as I have before, that anyone living that sort of life will not inherit the kingdom of God. But when the Holy Spirit controls our lives He will produce this kind of fruit in us: love, joy, peace, patience, kindness, goodness, faithfulness, Gentleness and self-control; and here there is no conflict with Jewish laws. Those who belong to Christ have nailed their natural evil desires to His cross and crucified them there. If we are living now by the Holy Spirit's power, let us follow the Holy Spirit's leading in every part of our lives" (Galatians 5:17-25, *Living Letters*).

"Your old evil desires were nailed to the cross with Him; that part of you that loves to sin was crushed and fatally wounded, so that your sin-loving body is no longer under sin's control, no longer needs to be a slave to sin; For when you are deadened to sin you are freed from all its allure and its power over you. And since your old sin-loving nature 'died' with Christ, we believe that you are now sharing His new life. Christ rose from the dead and will never die again. Death no longer has any power over Him. He died once for all to end sin's power, but now He lives forever in unbroken fellowship with God. So look upon your old nature as dead and unresponsive to sin and be alive instead to God, alert to Him, through

Jesus Christ our Lord. Do not let sin control you any longer; do not obey it; do not submit to it by giving in to its desires. Do not let any part of your bodies become tools of wickedness, to be used for sinning; but give yourselves completely to God — every part of you — for you are back from death and you want to be tools in the hands of God, to be used for His good purposes. Sin need never again be your master, for now you are no longer tied to the law where sin enslaves you, but you are free under God's favor and mercy" (Romans 6:6-14, *Living Letters*).

So there they are — ten obvious and significant lessons from Obadiah's twenty-one verses. May we learn them well and be the stronger thereby.

# BIBLIOGRAPHY

Robinson, G. L., *The Twelve Minor Prophets*. Grand Rapids, Michigan: Baker Book House.

Petrie, George, *Israel's Prophets*. Philadelphia: L. W. & D. B. Neal.

Morgan, G. Campbell, *The Minor Prophets*. Westwood, New Jersey: Fleming H. Revell Company.

Sampey, J. R., *Syllabus of Old Testament Study*. Nashville, Tennessee: Broadman Press.

Pfeiffer, Charles F., and Harrison, Everett F., "Wycliffe Bible Commentary." Chicago: Moody Press.

Eason, J. L., *Bible Survey*. Grand Rapids, Michigan: Zondervan Publishing House.

Farrar, F. W., *The Minor Prophets*. Anson, D. F. Randolph & Company.

Lewis, J. P., *The Minor Prophets*. Grand Rapids, Michigan: Baker Book House.

*Unger's Bible Handbook*. Chicago: Moody Press.

Brewer, J. A., "The International Critical Commentary." New York: Charles Scribner's Sons.

Calvin, John, "Commentaries on the Twelve Minor Prophets." Grand Rapids, Michigan: William B. Eerdmans Publishing Company.

Henry, Matthew, *Matthew Henry's Commentary*. Westwood, New Jersey: Fleming H. Revell Company.

Laetsch, T. F. K., "Bible Commentary," *The Minor Prophets*. St. Louis, Missouri: Concordia Publishing House.

Davidson, Stibbs & Kevan, "The New Bible Commentary." Grand Rapids, Michigan: William B. Eerdmans Publishing Company.

Gaebelein, A. C., *The Annotated Bible.* Our Hope Publishers.

Ironsides, Harry, *Notes on the Minor Prophets.* Neptune, New Jersey: Loizeux Brothers, Inc.

Smith, G. A., "The Expositor's Bible." Grand Rapids, Michigan: Zondervan Publishing House.

Schaff, P., "Lange's Commentary," *Old Testament.* Grand Rapids, Michigan: Zondervan Publishing House.

Elliott, C. J., "Layman's Handy Commentary." Grand Rapids, Michigan: Zondervan Publishing House.

Halley, H. H., *Bible Handbook.* Grand Rapids, Michigan: Zondervan Publishing House.